A BRIEF HISTORY OF FINLAND

MATTI KLINGE

A BRIEF HISTORY OF FINLAND

OTAVA
PUBLISHING COMPANY LTD
HELSINKI

First edition 1982

Illustrations chosen by the author
Translation: David Mitchell and Timothy Binham
Typography and layout: Sinikka Lindfors
Jacket design: Paavo Ojasti

Otava Printing Works
Keuruu 1997

ISBN 951-1-14789-7

Contents

Finland before 1155

Some ten thousand years ago, following the retreat of the continental ice-sheet, the first scattered settlements began to appear on the broad expanse of land, covered with lakes and forests, between the Gulf of Finland, the Gulf of Bothnia and Lake Ladoga. It is thought that the inhabitants of this area belonged racially and linguistically to the Finno-Ugrian group of peoples long before the Finns who gave their name to the country and its people migrated from the southern reaches of the Gulf of Finland to the south-western part of the Finnish peninsula at the beginning of the Christian calendar. But there is a difference, thousands of years old, between the inland and coastal areas of this region; it is reflected in the way of life of the people and in

An elkhead club from Huittinen in south-west Finland – about 5000 years old. Animal-head weapons of this sort, carved from soapstone, have been found in many parts of the country and far to the east.

their artifacts and is probably based on different racial and cultural traditions.

The important migration of peoples reached present Finland sometime prior to 3000 B.C. already; this migratory group which left behind combishly ornamented ceramic receptacles was apparently large, and its principal source of livelihood is presumed to have been sealing. Approximately between 1500 B.C. and 1000 A.D. contacts and migration took place essentially in the south whereby there was an influx into Finland of people, objects, terminology and other influences, the most significant of which was husbandry. Baltic influences came from the Estonian-Livonian region but also directly from the southernmost Lettish-Lithuanian area and subsequently the Western Slavic area, which again provided connections with the Black Sea and Mediterranean regions and later on with particularly the Eastern Roman Empire. The expansion of the Swedish settlement to Finnish coastal regions extends perhaps from the 9th century to the 14th century. The internal migration continued while Finland was part of the Kingdom of Sweden until 1809 and even further although Finland subsequently has been more a country of emigration than one of immigration. All migrations have brought along genes and cultural influences, and whereas the immigrants mostly have represented a higher cultural and technological standard, they have thus had a stronger effect on the structure of culture and society.

According to newest large-scale research based on the hereditary transmission of blood groups, about three quarters of the racial genic substance of the present Finnish people would be of western and southern origin, and one quarter of eastern origin;

whereby the western element is strongest in the west and in the coastal region to the effect that there is almost no difference to be noticed between the present Finnish-speaking and Swedish-speaking population of western Finland.

On the other hand, the linguistic structure of the modern nation shows that the eastern language has been stronger than the western and that a great many inhabitants of Germanic origin have adopted the various dialects of Finnish, with the apparent exception of the very latest arrivals from the west and their offspring. In respect of the language it must be emphasized, however, that although the (present) Finnish language forms a historical linguistic group together with Estonian and some Baltic minor languages and the languages of certain Russian inland tribes and peoples, as well as very remotely with Hungarian, the matter is different in consideration of other language grouping principles. The vocabulary of modern Finnish is largely of Germanic origin, and in view of their meaning, all abstract concepts, in particular, and the words relating to material objects and society conform as a result of historical and religious traditins etymologically to those of German and particularly Swedish.

The eastern expeditions of the Viking Age followed an important route which led in the shelter of the Finnish coastal archipelagos to the bayhead of the Gulf of Finland, to Lake Ladoga and from there, southwards along the waterways, as far as to Constantinople. The Vikings ruled in Novgorod in 862, in Kiev in 882 and, as early as 860, they had made their first attack on the capital of the eastern Roman Empire. According to runic stones many Swedes were still making journeys to Russia and Byzantium in the 10th and 11th centuries, some of them settling there. Inhabitants of the area now known as Finland certainly also participated in these expeditions, and Finnish and Baltic heathens continued their plundering raids to the east and the west even after the Scandinavian Viking expeditions had ended; the set of Sampo poems known from the Finnish national epic Kalevala can be presumed to relate to this tradition.

Linked to this period of transition, the conversion of the Nordic countries to Christianity and their incorporation into the European ecclesiastical and emerging political organization, is the entry of Finland into documented history and the sphere of social conditions reflected therein.

The Era of the Crusades

At the dawn of the historical era the area that later became Finland was not yet a united whole. The main tribes, the Finns proper, the Tavastians and the Karelians differed from each other in many respects and were often hostile to each other. The Finns had connections to the west and south, the Karelians to the south-east; furthermore, the Åland Islands and part of Western Finland and the archipelago had belonged since an earlier period to the Central Swedish military and economic system. In the 11th century expeditions were made from Sweden and Denmark to western Finland. They followed the old eastern route of the Vikings and were evidently also undertaken in competition with Novgorod. The Kingdom of Sweden, now coming into being with the Uppsala-Sigtuna district at its centre, sought to stabilize old economic and cultural links with western Finland. Tradition has it that the first crusade (around 1155), led by King Eric and St. Henry, the Bishop of Uppsala, was undertaken to extend the area of the Swedish influence. This was accomplished through the establishment of the Finnish Missionary Diocese headed by St. Henry. Missionary work was con-ducted towards Satakunda and along Kokemäki River further also to Tavastia.

The fact that St. Henry was of English origin links the establishment of the Finnish Missionary Diocese with the general development in Scandinavia. The Catholic Church came to Finland from England after attempts to introduce it from northern Germany had failed. Although there are virtually no written sources describing Finnish history in the 12th century, the scant historical eveidence that does exist, together with more plentiful arcaelogical findings, is sufficient to show that Christianity took

The frontispiece of the *Missale Aboense*, the missal of Turku diocese, printed in Lübeck in 1488. In the centre is Henry, the apostle of Finland and patron saint of Turku Cathedral, with his assassin, the Finnish farmer – or German trader? – Lalli at his feet. Kneeling on either side of the saint are Bishop Konrad Bitz and Maunu Särkilahti, Dean of Turku Cathedral, with their coats of arms. The memory of St. Henry was preserved in Finland in religious legend and imagery, and in the masterly folk epic known as *The Death of Henry*.

permanent root in south-western Finland and that religious, economic and political links developed between this area and Svealand and east Götaland. At the same time Novgorod was taking an open interest in the people and trading places along the shores of the Gulf of Finland and Lake Ladoga. This area too was united by religious, economic and political interests.

The Danes and Germans were also interested in the coastal regions along the old eastern route. Sweden failed in its attempt to gain influence in western Estonia and it was the King of Denmark who conquered the western and northern parts of the country and established Tallin in 1219. At the same time the Teutonic Knights were attempting to push northwards and gained temporary hold of Estonia but it was soon re-taken by the Danes. Meanwhile the second crusade, from Sweden into Tavastia, had taken place under the leadership of Earl Birger. With Sweden in control of Tavastia and the establishment of a castle there, the coast of eastern Uusimaa (Nyland) began to be settled by groups of Swedish immigrants. The centre of the area was probably Porvoo (Borgå). The aim behind these measures was to provide support for attempts at expansion towards the east. While the Mongolians attacked Russia from the east, the Swedish »Prince» and his troops, whose numbers included bishops as well as Finns and Tavastians, pushed their way as far as the River Neva. It was here in 1240 that they were defeated by Alexander Nevski, the Prince of Novgorod, who two years later defeated the Germans in Estonia.

In the 13th century a loosely defined border dividing Swedish and Novgorod interests took shape. It extended from the River Kymi through eastern Tavastia to a point somewhere on the coast of the Gulf of Bothnia. The decisive struggle for possession of the eastern coast of the Gulf of Finland and inland Finland was fought at the end of the 13th and beginning of the 14th centuries. In 1293 Sweden embarked on the third crusade and founded the Wiborg fortress and city. During an expedition undertaken in 1300, the Swedes founded the Landsk-

Turku Castle was a mighty centre of power and symbol of Swedish royal rule in Southwest Finland, or 'Finland Proper'. Enlarged over the centuries, in its heyday the castle housed the Renaissance-style court of John, Duke of Finland,

and his Polish wife Catharine Iagellonica. The rather naive 19th-century drawing contrasts the mundane figure of the fishing townsman with the crushing weight of history.

rona fortress on the banks of the River Neva, but this was destroyed by Novgorod. The long period of war came to an end with the Treaty of Pähkinäsaari (Schlüsselburg now Petrokrepost) in 1323. It was here that, for the first time, the border between Sweden and Novgorod (later Russia) was agreed; not only a political border, it was also to divide two religions and two cultures. The people of Savo and western Karelia, whom destiny had placed to the west of the border, were to grow up, alongside the Tavastians and Finns, within the political and cultural sphere of the Kingdom of Sweden and under the Roman Catholic Church. The Swedish settlements in Uusimaa and along the coastal areas of Karelia, the Wiborg and later the Olavinlinna fortresses, as well as the influence of trade and traders tied this area and its inhabitants to the West. Similarly, the Karelians, whom fate had placed east of the border, formed ever closer ties with Novgorod and the Orthodox Church. Later, the areas of North Karelia, Käkisalmi and the Karelian Isthmus were to be annexed to the Kingdom of Sweden and later still to the Finnish Grand Duchy. Thus the area, the people and the traditions that comprise modern Finland embrace Orthodox elements from east of the border as it was in the Middle Ages. However, the Finnish peninsula and its inhabitants were essentially linked to the emerging Swedish state and the Catholic Church. Indeed, the Karelians long referred to their western tribal brothers as »Swedes», a fact which demonstrates that, along the centuries, administrative and religious factors proved to be stronger than a common ancestry in the shaping of a nation's culture. The Finnish tribes, then, differed decisively from the Karelians and Estonians and joined the tribes of Sweden and the state growing up around them.

Part of the Kingdom of Sweden

In the Middle Ages, as part of the Kingdom of Sweden, Finland had no special status which might have been reflected in such things as a separate administration, different laws or an addition to the King's title. From the outset the Kingdom was essentially a community which had grown up around the sea and the waterways (Lake Mälare) leading to the sea. The sea was to remain the most important means of transport and communications until the era of the railways. Cultural, commercial and administra-tive development in the peasant Kingdom of Sweden and in the areas to the east and west of the sea were largely dependent on influences from further south. From the beginning of the 13th century onwards the country experienced a change of decisive importance when the early influence of the English Church was replaced by a German merchant and city-centred culture. At the same time members of the nobility from the south coast of the Baltic and even further afield moved into the country mostly to fill military and legal position. Estonia, the whole of which had come under the control of the Teutonic Knights in 1346 and whose capital had been predominantly German for some time, exerted a powerful influence throughout the Gulf of Finland area, as far as Turku and Stockholm. The influence of Sweden in the Middle Ages, on the other hand, can be seen clearly from the fact that only rarely did the families of the old local chieftains rise to the ranks of the nobility which had developed along with the system of castles and castle administration. On the other hand, the Swedish peasant settlements in Uusimaa and Ostrobothnia grew up, side by side, with the Finnish, creating a unified western Finnish culture despite the maintenance of two separate languages. This culture can be said, perhaps, to have

Most of the dozens of Finnish churches built of granite or brick in the Middle Ages have survived to our day. Many contain late mediaeval wall paintings, as the Reformation in Finland was largely untouched by iconoclastic fervour.

resembled that of eastern Sweden (Uppland – East Götaland) more than that of eastern Finland from which it differed in respect to traditions in agriculture, the family, artifacts and food.

An important feature of development in the 14th and 15th centuries was the way the Bishop's Seat in Turku, and their entire Church organization, established its position and thrived both spiritually and materially. As the ecclesiastical culture spread and took deeper root it tied Finland to the general sphere of European Christian culture. Gradually, stone churches, decorated with carvings and paintings, were built in all parts of inhabited Finland. The arrival in Finland of various monastic orders, including Dominicans, Franciscans, indigent orders and, later, the Order of St. Bridget, which took their place alongside the regular congregational clergy, strengthened the power of the Church. Journeys to the Papal curia in Avignon or Rome and, in particular, study trips to the famous universities on the continent, mainly to Paris, all of which formed part of the universal ecclesiastical culture of the Middle Ages, further advanced Finland's spiritual integration with Europe. Together with urban culture the influence of the church was felt specifically in the relatively densely populated areas of western Finland and was naturally weaker in those areas where, in addition to agriculture, life still revolved to a large extent round hunting trips and other forms of livelihood requiring mobility. The most important centres from which the new influences spread were Turku, with its Bishop's seat and Cathedral, and Wiborg, both of which were the home of a number of important figures of medieval bourgeois society, particularly members of the artisan professions. The people of these towns had close contacts with the bourgeois culture of Tallin, Stockholm, Danzig and Lübeck, a culture which in the Middle Ages was largely German orientated.

At the centre of the Kingdom the name Eastland was sometimes applied to Finland (Proper) and the other areas beyond the sea, evidently in the same way that Northland began to be used as a general name for the provinces to the north of the centre. Eastland and Northland formed important and organic links with the centre formed around Svealand and Götaland. In the 1350's and once more in the 1440's a common Law of the Land was drawn up. It was compiled on the basis of the old provincial laws. Such laws had been unknown in Finland and Northland. In about 1350 a general Town Law was also drawn up. Thus Swedish law and a Scandinavian social system became established in Finland. They were to remain permanent national characteris-tics, features which distinguish the culture of the Finns from that of the Karelians and the Esto-

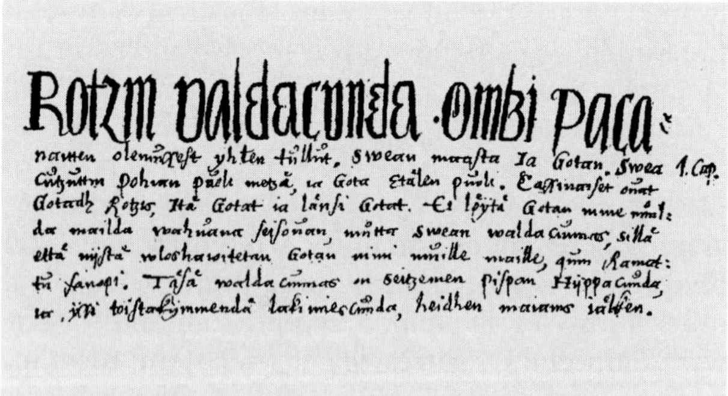
Rotzin valdacunda ombi paca:

The 16th-century translation into Finnish of the 1442 General Land Law of the Kingdom of Sweden begins with a description of the realm and a discussion of the significance of forests as borderlands.

The archaic fortified granite manor of the Flemings, a powerful Finnish family, at Parainen, in the southern archipelago of Turku. The location illustrates the primacy of water transport and the important defensive function of the manor.

nians. The right of representatives of the Finnish body of *lagman* (law-man = the country's highest magistrate) to participate in the election of the King was confirmed in 1362. This legal system, together with the four-estate representation (the nobility, the clergy, the burghers and the farmers) which had developed since the beginning of the 15th century, gave Finland indisputable and full political rights within the Kingdom of Sweden – unlike those countries which were defeated and annexed to the Kingdom later in the 16th and 17th centuries.

During the period of the Scandinavian (Kalmar) Union in the 15th and beginning of the 16th centuries, the influence of Denmark was felt in Finland too. Supporters of the Union and those opposed to it (they might better be described as opponents to each successive leader of the Union) met in open conflict, e.g. in the 1430's, the time of Engelbrekt Engelbrektsson and the 1470's, the period of Sten Sture the elder. Finland cannot be said to have formed a political entity or unit where this issue was concerned, but in practice it did function as an area of economic support, securing power for Sten Sture for example. If it is possible to talk of nationalistic feelings at that time, in Finland too they were directed against the Danes.

The Pähkinäsaari Treaty of 1323 did not put an end to the question of the Swedish Kingdom's eastern border. Its southern reaches, it is true, were clearly defined and placed the districts of Jääski and Äyräpää on the Karelian Isthmus in Swedish territory, but the third area mentioned by name in the Treaty, Savo, because of the nature of its settlements and the forms of livelihood practiced here, was not nearly so well defined. A semi-nomadic way of life and slash-and-burn agriculture, which meant the constant clearing of new land for cultivation, led to a complex system of ownership and property rights. The border ran northwards from the Karelian Isthmus to the sea, and it seems evident that there was a vast joint area of Swedish-Novgorodian dominance in the north where Swedish rights reached a borderline extending eastwards from the Karelian Isthmus to the Arctic Ocean whereas Russian rights reached a borderline extend-

The book published by Olaus Magnus in Venice gave great emphasis to the fact, marvellous to southern Europeans, that the sea and lakes freeze over in the winter, and that battles can be fought on the ice and goods transported over it.

The North had more to offer than just ice, winds, lakes and military prowess; it also produced sizable cereal crops, using particular farming techniques. A patch of forest was cleared and burned, after which the ashes produced two or three excellent harvests; then new land had to be cleared. There was plenty of uninhabited forest in Finland at the time – and much later.

ing westwards from the Karelian Isthmus to Central Ostrobothnia and the Gulf of Bothnia and partly into the territory of present Sweden. Until still much later, the major part of Lapland formed a common taxation area of two or even three powers. As permanent settlement and farming spread to this joint area of usufruct or taxation, conflicts arose over the borderline, and settlement became a form of land seizure. The Savo settlements spread out towards the east and, in the mid 1470's, the Lord of the Wiborg fortress, Erik Axelson Tott, built the Olavinlinna fortress on the border to provide support for expansion. The influence of Karelia-Novgorod was gradually pushed back from the coast of the Gulf of Bothnia. At all events, the districts of Pohjanmaa (Ostrobothnia) and Länsipohja (Westrobothnia) were deemed part of the Kingdom of Sweden in 1346 when the border between the Uppsala and Turku diocese was fixed as running between the River Kemi and the River Kaakama. Thus, by virtue of its expanding settlements, Sweden gained considerable areas to the east of the border as it was defined in the Treaty of Pähkinäsaari, a fact which led to continuous border conflicts. Sweden ignored the continuous demands of Novgorod that it should mark out its border in the terrain. When the border was eventually re-drawn at the Peace Treaty of Täyssinä (1595), it more or less followed the eastern limits to the Savo settlements, a border which had in fact been established in practice much earlier and which, by continuing to the Arctic Sea, also confirmed Swedish (and Danish) supremacy in Lapland.

THE BIRTH OF THE CENTRALIZED STATE

The collapse of the Scandinavian Union and the reign of Gustavus I Vasa (1523–1560) represented an important turning point in the history of the Swedish state and especially of its eastern territories.

Separation from Denmark and Norway on the one hand, and the Reformation, with its financial ex-ploitation of the Church, on the other, led to Sweden's cultural isolation from the rest of Europe, with which it had become united in the international atmosphere of the 15th century. The trend to a more provincial culture, following the general principles of the Reformation, meant the appearance in Sweden of literature in both languages of the state, with the Bible translated into Swedish and (most of it) into Finnish. Other ecclesiastical and legal works also appeared in both languages. In translating such works into Finnish, Michael Agricola, rector of the Cathedral school in Turku, who had studied under Luther and Melanchton at Wittenberg and would eventually become Bishop of Turku, laid the basis for a Finnish literature. Following the Reformation, with Gustavus Vasa's expropriation of church property, there was little support for advances in the field of culture. The state profited considerably from the »nationalization» of the Church. In the Kingdom now separated from Denmark, Finland held a position of real importance, a fact reflected in the role played by members of the Finnish nobility in state administration and the army in the 16th century.

During the reign of Gustavus Vasa the country's economic structure underwent a decisive change

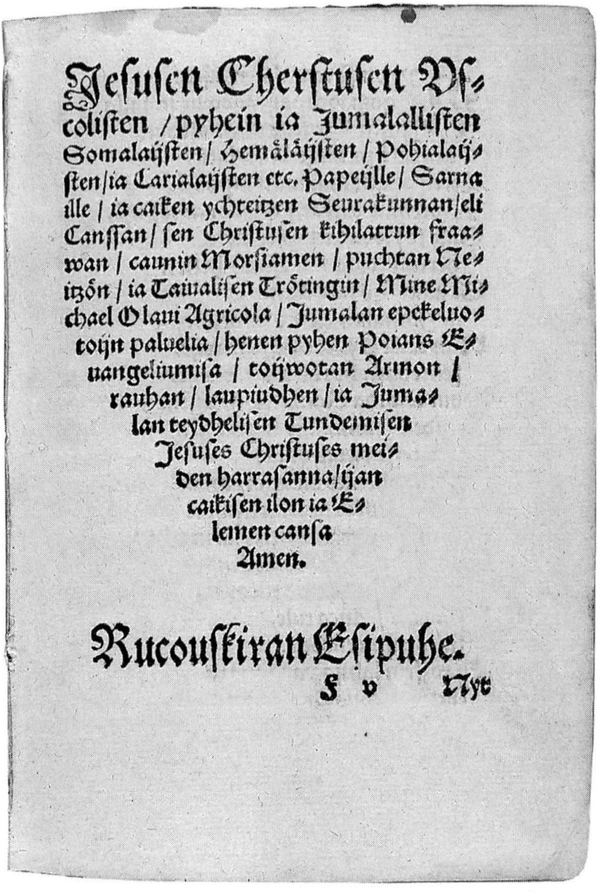
Jeſuſen Cherſtuſen Aſ-
coliſten / pyhein ia Jumalalliſten
Somalaiſten / Hemäläiſten / Pohialai-
ſten / ia Carialaiſten etc. Papeille / Sarna-
ille / ia caiken ychteiſen Seurakunnan / eli
Canſſan / ſen Chriſtuſen kihilattun fraa-
wan / caunin Morſiamen / puchtan Ne-
itzön / ia Taiwaliſen Tröſtingin / Mine Michael Olaui Agricola / Jumalan epekeluo-
toijn paluelia / henen pyhen Poians E-
uangeliumiſa / toijwotan Armon /
rauhan / laupiudhen / ia Jumalan teydheliſen Tundemiſen
Jeſuſes Chriſtuſes mei-
den harraſanna / ijan
caikiſen ilon ia E-
lemen canſa
Amen.

Rucouſkiran Eſipuhe.

F v Nyt

Master Michael Agricola, a pupil of Luther's and later Bishop of Turku, translated into Finnish and edited an impressive corpus of works in the 1540s, comprising the whole New Testament and much of the Old Testament, and several religious manuals for the clergy. The most notable of these was the encyclopedic *Rukouskirja Bibliasta* (Book of Prayers from the Bible), the finest product of 16th-century Humanist learning in the entire kingdom of Sweden.

with taxation and financial administration, previously based on a system of castle *fiefs*, now the direct responsibility of the centralized state. The financial difficulties of the Crown, which led to the almost complete confiscation of Church property, was also behind the proclamation of 1542 claiming the uninhabited wilds of Finland as Crown property. This paved the way for extensive state-controlled territorial expansion, particularly in Savo where settlements built around the method of slash-and-burn agriculture spread hundreds of kilometres to the north and north-west.

Throughout the 16th century, right up until the Peace Treaty of Stolbova in 1617, Sweden's political relations with Russia played a central part in the country's affairs. Behind this was not only dissatisfaction with the border as it was defined at Pähkinäsaari but also changes within Russia, the Baltic and Poland. The war with Russia (1555–57) ended with neither side having achieved a clear victory. With the collapse of the Teutonic Knights in 1561, Tallin allied itself with Sweden, but throughout the 1570's fierce battles were fought with Russia both in Estonia and in Finland. Swedish victories between 1580 and 1581, particularly those at Käkisalmi and Narva, led to the addition of »Grand Duke of Finland, Karelia, Ingria and a fifth part of Vatja (Käkisalmi)» to King John III's title. These successes were due in part to the fact that Russia was being harassed by Poland at the same time.

With his marriage to Catherine Jagellonica in 1563, John III had already strengthened Sweden's ties with Poland. The marriage produced a son, Sigismund, who became king of both Sweden and Poland.

In 1593 the clergy and also the other estates convened in Uppsala for a kind of parliamentary session at which Lutheranism was finally and definitely approved as the one and only established state religion. The Kingdom assumed from then on also features of a clerical state since the duties of the clergy were very comprehensive in the extensive pro-vinces until the late 19th century; both the spiritual and educational and to a great extent also the econo-mical and administrative leadership was mainly en-trusted to the vicars. The clergy had already earlier constituted an estate of the realm, and in the Lutheran world, where clergymen lead a married life, the clergy became a hereditary estate similar to the nobility.

A civil war broke out later when Sigismund's uncle, Charles, the Duke of Södermanland, took up the cause of Protestantism and the centralized state in opposition to Sigismund who was supported by the Catholics and the higher nobility and who favoured a more old-fashioned type of decentralized state controlled by the latter. The Finnish Governor, Klaus Fleming, and most of the Finnish nobility supported the King in this dispute and were later to pay for this when the Duke won the war and became King Charles IX. In what is known as the Club (i.e. cudgel) War (1596–97), Charles was supported by the peasants of Ostrobothnia, Tavastia and Savo, who were discontented with the deterioration in social conditions and therefore rose up in rebellion. The rebellion, however, was put down by Klaus Fleming.

During the reign of Gustavus II Adolphus, son of Charles IX, war with Russia broke out once more with the states bordering on Russia attempting to take advantage of the country's internal disorder.

During this war, which ended in 1617, Sweden annexed Ingria and the province of Käkisalmi, areas which it had temporarily held earlier. This left Russia com-pletely cut off from the Baltic Sea.

The 16th century was characterized by attempts to strengthen the position of the Crown and to centralize state administration. So succesfully did Gustavus Vasa augment his position that in 1544 the system of elected kings was replaced with an hereditary monarchy. The centralization of tax collection and state finances made for considerable conformity, a development which was further strengthened by the transference to the state of the power and property of the Church. The struggle for power which followed when Gustavus Vasa bestowed Dukedoms on his sons (John was given the Duchy of Finland, i.e. the south-western part of the country, where, for a short period, he held what was for the times a magnificent Renaissance court in the Turku Castle) held back attempts at centralization. A struggle for power between the King and members of the higher nobility as well as a peasant rebellion brought about by the burden of a new administration and war machinery were common features in Europe at this time. As the Crown grew in strength it attempted to turn the nobility, which was a more or less independent local gentry, into a body of civil servants and military officials. The execution of many of Sigismund's followers went a long way towards breaking the power of the nobility.

On the other hand, the con-tinuous wars tended to stress the significance of the nobility, and by rewarding succesful military leaders with prizes of land a kind of post-feudal situation was brought about. The change in the position of the nobility can be seen from the fact that, whereas in the latter

The Finnish coat of arms goes back to the days of King John III of Sweden. The flag in the funeral procession bears the initials I. R., Iohannes Rex. The royal bearings and the heraldic status of the Duchy of Finland reflected the eastward expansion of the Swedish kingdom: wishing to assert itself vis-à-vis Russia and Poland, the Vasa family, still a newcomer to the Swedish throne, added a new item to the list of royal titles. The message lies in the placing of the two swords in the bearings; the curved sabre may originally have been a reference to the Turks, but it soon came to be associated with the Russians.

During the 17th century, the nation's elite flocked to Stockholm, which established its position as the royal capital. Nonetheless, a handful of Baroque mansions were built in Finland, too. In the 19th century Louhisaari Manor, which originally belonged to the Fleming family, came into the hands of the Mannerheims, a family representing the new aristocracy. Gustaf Mannerheim, Marshal of Finland, was born there in 1865.

part of the 16th century a number of Finland's leading families, including the Flemings and the Horns, had palatial mansions built, in the 17th century, with the exception of the Fleming family's Louhisaari and the Creutz' Sarvilahti, such extravagant family manors were not built at all in Finland. The powerful figures of the country tended to build their manors and palaces in or around Stockholm.

From the reign of Gustavus II Adolphus onwards, a characteristic feature of Sweden's period as a great power was the fact that, at first the Baltic countries, then Poland and finally Germany took the place of Russia as objects of Sweden's military and political ambitions. The wars in Germany were fought mainly with native Swedish manpower and this placed a considerable strain on the country's economy and population. This period of military activity, together with involvement in the wars on the continent, enhanced the position of the military leaders, that is to say the nobility. The Regency governments and the favourable attitudes of Queen Christina increased still further the prestige of the nobility. Many of those areas whose taxes were distributed as rewards for military achievements in the form of *fiefs* were located in Ostrobothnia and Karelia.

The entire Bible was published in Finnish in 1642 in a handsome illustrated edition, with the portrait of the young Queen Christina on the frontispiece. The only child of Gustavus II Adolphus »the Great», Christina had not yet come of age at the time, and only began to rule two years later. The University of Finland (today the University of Helsinki) was founded during Christina's reign in 1640. The Treaty of Westphalia, which put an end to the prolonged wars that had raged throughout Europe, was concluded on terms favourable to Sweden in 1648. Christina's reign was a time of political and intellectual Europeanization for Sweden. The Queen herself converted to Catholicism and abdicated, spending the remainder of her life mostly in Rome. The portrait is framed by the coats of arms of all the Swedish provinces, with that of the »Duchy of Finland» (in its present-day form) flanking the principal bearings. The duchy was of purely heraldic significance, and had no separate administration of its own.

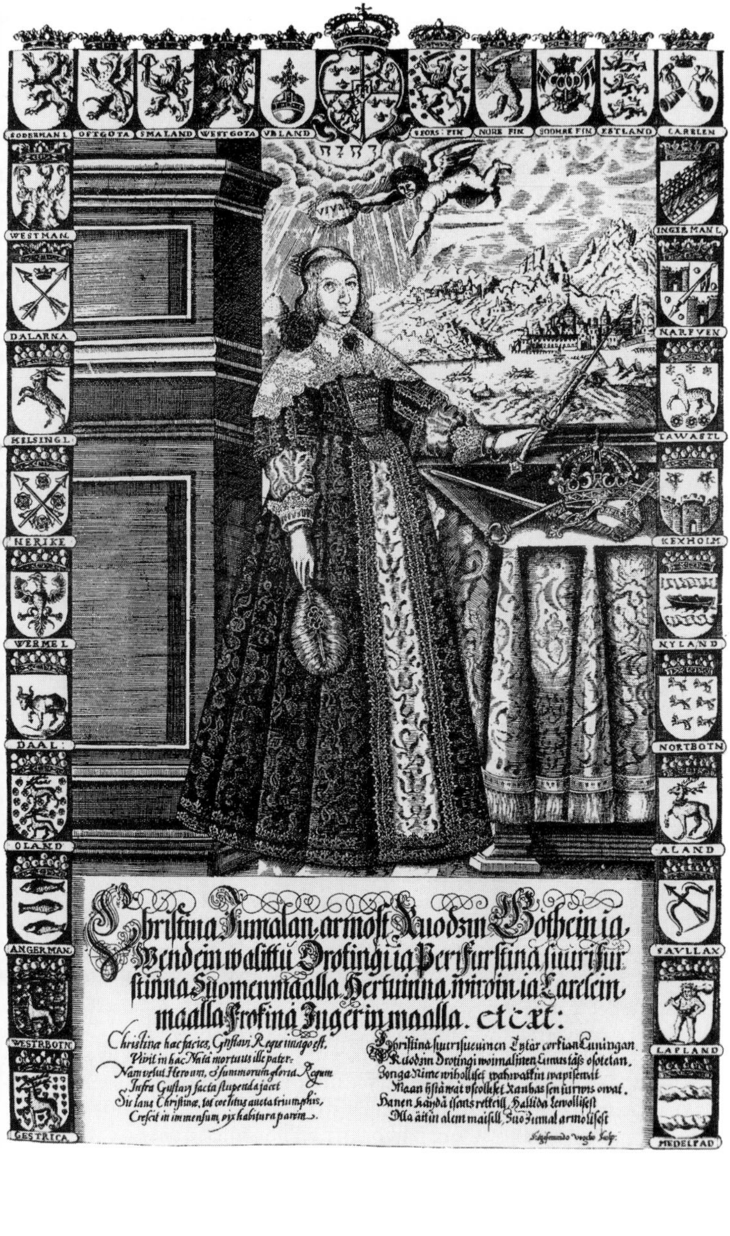
SODERMANL
OSTGOTA
SMALAND
WESTGOTA
VBLAND
SFORS: FIN
NORE FIN
SODHRE FIN
ESTLAND
CARELEN
VIVAT
WESTMAN
INGERMANL
DALARNA
NARFVEN
HELSINGL
TAWASTL
NERIKE
KEXHOLM
WERMEL
NYLAND
DAAL
NORTBOTN
OLAND
ALAND
ANGERMAN
SAVLLAX
WESTRBOTN
LAPLAND
GESTRICA
MEDELPAD
Christina Jumalan armost Ruodzin Gothein ia Wendein walittu Drotingi ia Peri Furstina suuri Fur stinna Suomenmaalla Hertuinna Wiroin ia Carelein maalla Frokina Ingerin maalla. etc.xt:
Christina hac facies, Gustavi Regis imago est,
Vivit in hac Nata mortuus ille pater:
Nam velut Heroum, & summorum gloria Regum
Infra Gustavi facta stupenda jacet
Sic laus Christinæ, tot coelitus aucta triumphis,
Crescit in immensum, vix habitura parem.
Christina suuri suuruinen Tytär corkian Cuningan
Ruodzin Drotingi woimalinen Cunnias täss osotetan,
Jonga Nimte wihollisel wahwattin wapisewat
Maan hstäwät ystolliset Xanhas sen surwis owat.
Hanen kandä isäns retkeill, Hallida lewollisest
Ylla äitin alem maisill, Suo Jumal armollisest

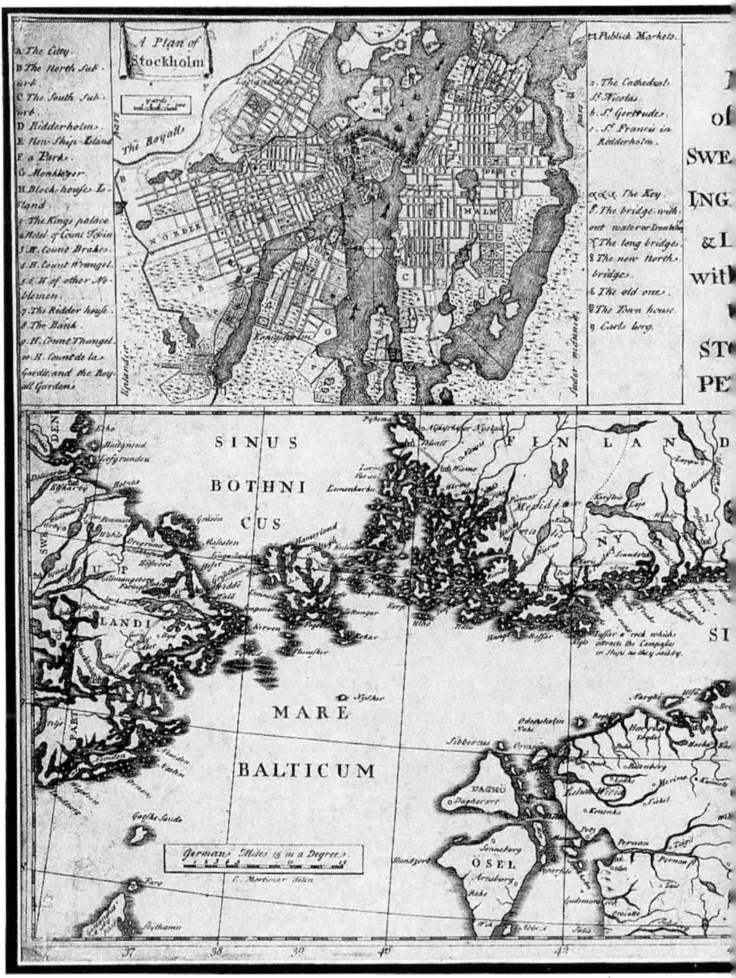

This late 18th-century map illustrates Finland's position in the dynamics between the two metropolises, Stockholm and St. Petersburg. Founded in 1703, only a hundred years later, St. Petersburg had over a million inhabitants, and the city's defence became the cornerstone of Russian

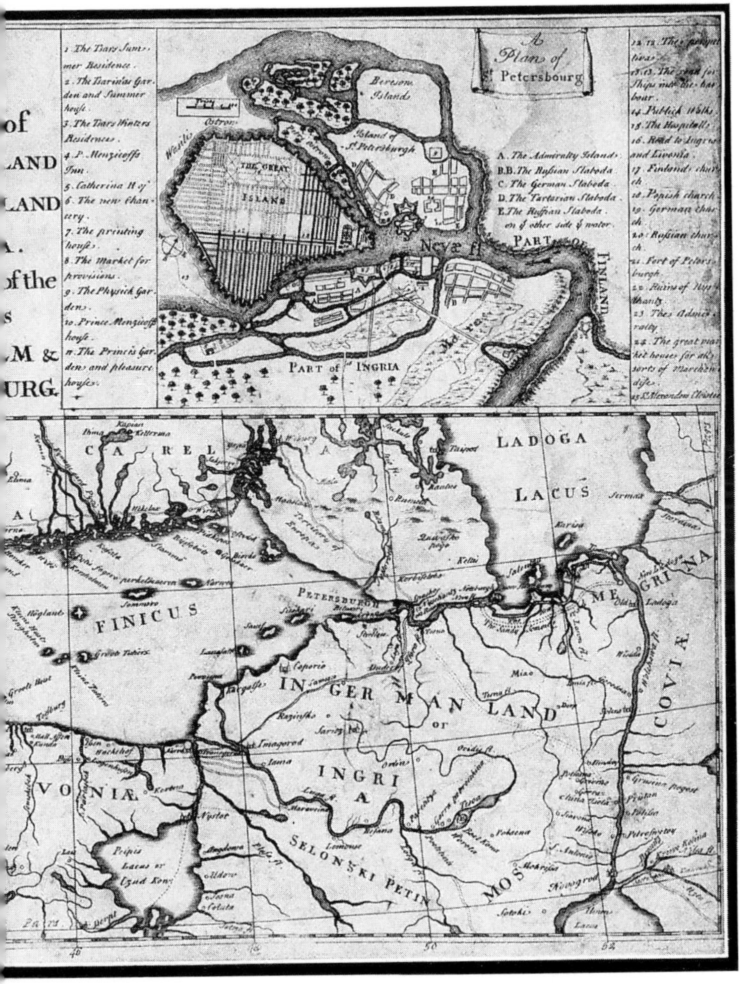

military strategy. In 1710 Russia wrested the south coast of the Gulf of Finland from Sweden, in 1808 the north coast as well. In the years 1917–1920 Finland and Estonia broke away from Russia, but Estonia was again under Russian rule from 1940 to 1991.

Procession on the occasion of the founding in 1640 of the University of Finland in Turku; painting in the assembly hall of the University of Helsinki. The original painting by Albert Edelfelt was destroyed in the Russian bombing of Helsinki in 1944.

Another development during this period was the increasing importance attached to the position of Stockholm. With Stockholm the final home of central administration and with the Diet firmly rooted there through the erection of the first parlia-

ment building, the House of Nobility, the town exerted an influence on all parts of the Kingdom. Stockholm's position was also strengthened by a mercantile economic policy, one expression of which was the banning of foreign trade in towns along the Gulf of Finland and Gulf of Bothnia in favour of the capital. Thus the country's period as a great power saw the creation of a firmer administrative unity, a development that was felt in all walks of life.

During this period the main centres of popula-

Quod benè vertat Altissimus
COLLEGII ETHICI
DISP. XIII. & ULTIMA
De
AMICITIA
QUAM
In Regiâ ad Auram Universitate
SUB PRÆSIDIO
VIRI Nobilissimi atq; Consultissimi
DN. MICHAELIS Gyllenstålpe
WEXIONII, J. U. & Phil. D. perexîmij,
Jur. Polit. & Hist. P. P. celeberrimi,
Præceptoris & promotoris sui
summè devenerandi.
Liberalis exercitij ergò defendendam suscipit
In audit. sup: die Jun. 20. Ann. 165–
GREGORIUS GR. ARCTOPOLITANUS FINLANDUS.
ABOÆ
Imprimebat Petrus Hansson/ *Acad. Typog.*

I. N. J.
IN VERBA PHOCYLLIDÆ
De
QUATUOR
GENERIBUS
MULIERUM,
COMMENTATIO,
Quam
SUB FORMA DISPUTATIONIS
Venia Ampl. Fac. Phil. in Acad. ad Auram,
PRÆSIDE
Viro Clarissimo
M. CHRISTIERNO
ALANDRO,
Eloqventiæ Professore Regio & Ord.
h. t. Decano spectabili,
Præceptore & Promotore, summa animi
reverentia ætatem observando.
Speciminis loco,
Publico examini modeste sistit
LAURENTIUS N. QWIST/
Biörneburgensis,
In Audit. Max. die 20 Aprilis, A. 1698.
Impr. apud Jo. LAURENTII WALLIUM.

1915—1916
JEAN SIBELIUS
esittää uusimmat
SÄVELLYKSENSÄ
Yliopiston Juhlasalissa
Keskiviikkona Jouluk. 8 p:nä 1915 k:lo ½ 8 i. p.
AVUSTAA: KAUPUNGINORKESTERI.

OHJELMA:
1. **Aallottaret** (Okeaniidit) Sävelruno orkesterille, op. 73.
2. **Serenata I** (D-duuri) } viulusoololle ja orkesterille, op. 69: a, b.
Serenata II (G-molli) }

VÄLIAIKA

3. **Sinfonia V** (Ess-duuri) op. 82.
Tempo tranquillo assai. Quasi attacca al
Allegro comminciando moderato e poco a poco stretto
Andante mosso
Allegro commodo Largamente molto.

tion and the economic hub of the Kingdom of Sweden were situated around the waterways along the line Gothenburg–Stockholm–Turku–Tallin–Wiborg. At the beginning of the 17th century the emphasis was further to the east than it would be later, as is indi-cated by the fact that the two universities established after that of Upsala were situated in Tarto (1632) and Turku (1640). Income received from Estonia and Lithuania was of considerable importance to the Kingdom. The composition of the ruling class was also altered with the intake of nobility from the Baltic countries. During the 1630's, with the war being waged for the most part in the south, the southern reaches of the Kingdom gained in impor-tance and the inclusion in the realm of wealthy provinces seized from Denmark in 1658 meant that the country's centre of gravity shifted further west and further south. But it was not until the 18th century that Finland became a more peripheral region within the Kingdom. This was due, on the one hand, to the powerful growth of Gothenburg and trade with the west, and on the other, and this was more important, to Russian

Thousands of master's theses directed by professors of history, philosophy and rhetoric were published by the University of Helsinki, mostly on moral questions. Some of these disputations were actually written by the professors and defended by their students. One such thesis, *De amicitia* (On Friendship), is depicted here. Others, such as *De quatuor generibus mulierum* (The Four Types of Women), were written by the students themselves. Professors also wrote other books, such as this volume by Achrelius on the writing of letters. The purpose was to implant Continental Renaissance Humanism in Finland.

Stockholm was the seat of government for the Finns until 1809, from which time Helsinki was developed as a separate Finnish capital city. Turku was an important provincial centre, the main seat of the Catholic Church in Finland in the Middle Ages; still today, the primate of the Finnish Church resides there. Viipuri in the east rivalled Turku as Finland's second major provincial centre.

expansion westwards since the time of Peter the Great.

The establishment of a university (1640) and a Court of Appeals (1623) in Turku, the publication in Finnish of the complete Bible (1642) and the appearance of several new towns gives some indication of developments in Finland in the 17th century, a period during which the country was, on several occasions, to enjoy the status of a special area of administration, Count Per Brahe, did much to advance the country's position. In being placed under the administration of a Governor-General, Finland was not, in fact, treated as a special case within the Kingdom, as other parts of the realm were also liable to be temporarily grouped into a district of special administration. During his first period of office, Brahe's area of administration comprised Finland and the province of Käkisalmi but not Ostrobothnia while his second covered Finland and Ostrobothnia without the province of Käkisalmi. This is one indication of the fact that the name Finland had not yet taken on its present meaning.

There was a good deal of migration between the various parts of the Kingdom, and this had its effect on the relationship between the two languages. Since the Middle Ages Finns from the west had been moving into Sweden and at the beginning of the 17th century large numbers of people migrated from Savo to western Sweden, where they gradually became absorbed into the Swedish-speaking population. Furthermore, centralization and the increased significance of Stockholm tended to strengthen the position of the Swedish language in Finland. Now and then, however, some attention was paid to the question of the ability of authorities in the Finnish-speaking area to use Finnish, and in the 18th century a translator was appointed to the Diet (the legislative assembly) for the benefit of the peasant representa-tives. In Stockholm, alongside the *Storkyrkan,* the Capital's most important church, there was also a Finnish church, which in fact still functions to this day. But it must be pointed out that, as the language of the Court and the nobility, German held an important position, as did Latin in University life.

RUSSIAN EXPANSION WESTWARDS IN THE 18THCENTURY

Changes along the eastern border, tension and a relative decline in her importance within the Kingdom were features central to developments in Finland during the 18th century. As Russia grew in strength it began to expand to the west and in 1703 St. Petersburg was founded on territory that was still formally part of Sweden. In the Great Northern War which began in 1700, Russia occupied Estonia and Lithuania in addition to Ingria and Karelia and, from 1710 onwards, the whole of Finland as far as the Åland Islands and was even threatening the archipelago around Stockholm. The period of occupation, which was to be known as the Great Wrath, came to end with the Peace of Uusikaupunki (Nystad) in 1721 and with it came a redefinition of the Kingdom's eastern border and for Finland (without Karelia) once more under Swedish rule, a more peripheral position than before.

Following the major famine of the 1690's, a long war and a period of occupation, Finland's popu-

From ancient times, the strategic importance of the Gulf of Finland has prompted the construction of fortifications and defences. The mighty fortress of Sveaborg was built from 1748 onwards, largely with French funds, on seven islands off the coast at Helsinki. About the same time, Sweden built a modern, fast and powerful galley fleet well suited to naval warfare in the Gulf archipelago.

lation and agriculture were in a poor state but, after the Treaty of Uusikaupunki, rural areas experienced a rapid revival, particularly the agricultural sector. The population of the area later to be known as Finland was about 390 000 in 1721, but by 1807 it had grown to 907 000. Development in the towns and in urban occupations was much slower. Despite a great number of new farms there was a rapid

increase in the landless population and social divisions began to appear with a tenantfarmer class emerging on the one hand and a group of wealthy peasants and *rusthollis* (holder of a farm under obligation to furnish and equip a cavalryman) on the other. Particularly towards the latter half of the 18th century there was a general improvement in the standard of living and this was naturally reflected in the sphere of culture.

During the war of reprisal known as the War of the Hats, between 1741 and 1743, Finland was once more occupied by Russia. Under the Treaty of Turku (1743), with the new border drawn along the River Kymi, Finland lost the Olavinlinna fortress along with the towns of Lappeenranta and Hamina, the latter of which had been built up as a port and fortress town to replace Wiborg, ceded to Russia under the Treaty of Uusikaupunki. At this time the idea was already being expressed that Finland should break away from Sweden. However, after the war, measures were taken to strengthen Finland's position within the realm, prominent among which were an economic development programme and the building of fortifications and naval fleet. The construction of Sveaborg (Viapori in Finnish, nowadays Suomenlinna) outside of Helsinki was a huge financial enterprise. Its very name indicates its wide national function. Economically and culturally Finland formed closer and closer links with Stockholm. Along with improvements in the standard of living and culture and better communications the Swedish language became more general. The effect of internal migration was felt particularly in the towns along the coast. A body of Finnish literature, mostly ecclesiastical and legal in nature, began to appear and for a short period a Finnish-language newspaper was published. The position of the Finnish language was recognized in the Diet and on bank notes, etc. but the increasing importance of the western parts of the Kingdom, including Gothenburg, pushed the whole of Finland and consequently the Finnish language into a more peripheral position. This was the main reason for the fact that the Finnish civil service became continously more Finnish, that is to say that fewer and fewer officials came to Finland from other parts of the Kingdom.

The Regency, which reached the peak of its power towards the end of the 17th century, was superseded by the power of the Estates, the »Age of Freedom», which, in turn, came to an end with Gustavus III's coup d'état in 1772. The reign of Gustavus III and Gustavian culture were to be of importance to Finland and the reaffirmation of the

Gustavus III rose to the Swedish throne in 1771 and began to implement a tolerant but effective reform programme in Sweden (and Finland), similar to that his maternal uncle Frederick the Great had carried out in Prussia. In the following year, the king succeeded in decisively restricting the power of the Diet, which was run by the nobility. This ultimately led to his assassination at a masked ball at the Royal Opera in Stockholm in 1792 – a subject later adapted by Verdi. The reign of Gustavus III saw the breakthrough in Sweden of French civilization and Italian classicism and art, while the kingdom gathered economic and military strength.

In 1789 and 1790, two major naval battles – the latter being the biggest ever fought in the Baltic Sea – were fought in the Gulf of Finland near the present-day town of Kotka. The first battle was won by Sweden, the second by Russia; the outcome of the war was that the old borders remained unchanged. The wars against Russia coincided with crises in Russian–Turkish relations, as Sweden sought to profit from Russia's engagement in the south. France allied itself with Turkey in these wars; the two countries had a common enemy in the Habsburg monarchy.

power of the Regency was regarded as serving Finnish interests better than the power of the Diet. However, the nobility gradually rose up in opposition to the King as he began to limit the power of the Diet, simultaneously favouring those Estates of lower economic status. This development reached its peak in 1789 with the Act of Union and Security which was in the nature of a constitution and which

The Finnish interior at the time of the war of 1788; St. Olaf's Castle (i.e. Savonlinna, famed today for its international opera festivals), a fortress built on the border between Sweden and Russia in the 15th century, looms in the background.

The industrialization of Finland began with iron. Although there was some ore in Finland, its real riches were timber and water power; in fact, most of the ore was brought from the Stockholm archipelago by ship. The Fagervik ironworks community, complete with manor and church, near the Uusimaa coast.

the King sprang on the Diet as a kind of *fait accompli* in the middle of the war against Russia (1788–90).

During this war, which also developed into a war against Denmark, a separatist movement among army offices, with its roots in the opposition formed by the nobility, attempted to force the King to make peace by conducting separate negotiations with Russia. The origins of this officers' revolt (they were called the Anjala League) lay partly in plans, outlined a few years earlier by G. M. Sprengtporten, for an independent Finland under Russian suzerainty: these plans envisaged a nobility-centred form of government, based on ideas from the United States of America, resembling the Diet of the Age of Freedom. While they probably played a part in the way Finland's position would be organized between 1808 and 1809, these plans received little support during the war of 1788–1790.

But it is difficult to draw parallels between Finland's position as it was envisaged under Russian rule, with its government of nobles, and the reality of the country's subsequent history. Behind these events, which were tied up with the Anjala League, was the broad national constitutional opposition of the nobility to the power of the Regency. On the other hand, from Russia's point of view the plans to separate Finland from Sweden were of great significance. Following the subsequent Finnish war (1808–1809), fought against the background of the European power politics of the Napoleonic era, occupied Finland was no longer handed back to Sweden as it had been in 1721 an 1743, but was annexed by Russia as an autonomous »buffer state» with its own Diet and administration; Russia had, in fact, already considered the establishment of such a Diet during earlier periods of occupation in the 18th century. However, as the war indicates, there was a great deal of opposition to partition in Sweden and Finland. The reasons for Finland's separation from Sweden were not based on ethnical or linguistic principles or on the kind of nationalistic grounds that would appear later, neither was the border between Sweden and Russia (the Finnish Grand Duchy) drawn up on the basis of ethnic-linguistic considerations. It was not until after 1809 that a sense of Finnish identity began to develop, a trend which was later to embrace the kind of antiquarian interest that H. G. Porthan and his friends and pupils were to show in Finnish history, folklore and language during the latter part of the 18th century when the influence of the old University of Turku had been at its peak.

The Autonomous Grand Duchy

In signing the Treaty of Tilsit in 1807, Czar Alexander I of Russia and Napoleon had come to an agreement on their respective spheres of interest, after which Russia had conquered Finland (1808–1809). Finland was of strategic importance to Russia because of its proximity to St. Petersburg. A hundred years earlier Peter the Great had conquered Karelia, Estonia and Lithuania and had founded his Capital on the territory he had taken. It was logical, therefore, to attempt to make the entire Gulf of Finland inaccessible to enemy fleets. Russia's front line of defence was brought up from Kronstadt to the Sveaborg (Suomenlinna) fortifications and even further to the west. In the 1830's work was begun on what was planned to be the major fortification of Bomarsund on the Åland Islands. With its sparse population and its poverty, Finland as such did not interest Russia, but the establishment of St. Petersburg had made it necessary to protect its western capital and ensure access to the Baltic Sea. Sweden, its period as a great power at an end, no longer constituted any great danger, but what Russia did consider a danger was the possibility that during a major war Sweden, or later an independent Finland, by forming alliances with Russia's enemies, would provide them with a base from which to attack. It was Sweden's alliance with Great Britain, the enemy of France and Russia (now enjoying friendly relations), that was behind the war of 1808–1809.

A very important aspect of Russia's annexation of Finland was the way in which it was carried out and the form that Finnish society assumed as a result. As such, it was not exceptional that Finland was allowed to retain its own legislation and its own form of society since many other countries annexed by Russia earlier, including the Baltic states, had kept their own forms of government and in 1815 Poland too retained its status as a separate kingdom within the Russian Empire. Finland's position was con-firmed, with the war still in progress, at the grand Duchy's first separate Diet held in Porvoo, at which time the Czar proclaimed Finland's »elevation to the national status». Russia was not a united centralized state, neither was it united nationally or religiously. Thus, from the Russian point of view there was nothing peculiar or exceptional in Finland's Lutheran Church. However, in relation to Russia, Finland's position regarding its internal affairs was one of considerable independence, evidently for the reason that, in certain respects, it served as a model area from the point of view of the liberal policies that Alexander I was pursuing at the time. The free status of the Finnish peasantry and their representation in the Diet was of particular importance to Alexander and his plans to carry out reforms throughout the Realm, plans which were interrupted by Napoleon's attack in 1812. Finland not only retained its Lutheran religion, Swedish as its official language, its old Swedish system of civil and criminal law, but also its Gustavian form of government, the adaptation of which to Finnish circumstances together with the fact that Finland had its own central administration headed by the Senate and, in principle, its own Diet with its four Estates, meant the birth of a separate Finnish state. Finland had, of old, held the heraldic status of a Grand Duchy, now it became a Grand Duchy de facto, with its own insitution. The autocratic Czar of Russia agreed, by way of an»experiment» to become the constitutional monarch of Finland and Poland. From here it was intended that this system be extended to cover the whole of Russia. However, due to changing circumstances in Europe this did not materialize and, as a result of the uprisings in 1830 and 1863, Poland lost its Parliament and its special status. The Finns, who remained loyal and rather conservative throughout the 19th century, had what were on the whole rather favourable conditions to develop a state which had come into being as the result of Great power politics and which, although it did not constitute an ethnic totality, was nevertheless a geographically viable entity. Dialects of Finnish were spoken on both the Swedish and Russian sides of the border and, in Finland itself, in addition to the Swedish-speaking or bilingual upper classes, there was considerable Swedish-speaking rural population. Alexander had wanted the state to include the Swedish-speaking Åland Islands but not the Finnish-speaking area of Länsipohja (Westrobothnia); what was involved was the forming of a strategic and not expressly an ethnic entity. As far as trade and communications were concerned, western Finland inclined towards Sweden, eastern Finland more and more towards St. Petersburg. Later, the network of roads and canals, and partiularly the coming of the railroad, would support the tendency of administration to centralize in a way counter to the disintegrative hull of these major commercial centres.

A clear indication of Russia's desire to make an independently functioning entity of Finland was the creation of the area's own capital. Under Swedish rule, Turku, with its Bishop's Seat, its University and its Court of Appeals, had been the centre of the province, but Finland's capital had, of course, been Stockholm. Now, with the decision to make Helsinki the new administrative centre, (1812), a new capital

The Imatra Rapids cut a gash through the geological ridge formation known as Salpausselkä. To the north of the ridge lies Finland's most extensive lake district. During the romantic 19th century, the rapids were a renowned tourist draw, attracting visitors particularly from St. Petersburg. The waters

of the Finnish lakes discharge via the rapids into Lake Ladoga and from there via the River Neva into the sea at St. Petersburg. The Saimaa Canal, which connects a navigable lake route over 400 kilometres long with the Gulf of Finland at Viipuri, was built somewhat west of Imatra in 1856.

Conquered by Russia in 1809, Finland was turned into an autonomous Grand Duchy with its own political institutions and capital city. The centre of Helsinki was built in Grecian style. Architect C. L. Engel produced an elegant combination of Berlin Neo-Humanism and St. Petersburg tradition. The result, well-suited to the Neo-Humanist leanings of Finnish academic circles, reflected Russia's political ambitions in the Balkans.

was created. Helsinki had been burnt down during the war and now it was re-built in an unprecedentedly handsome fashion to show both Finns and the outside world that a new political unit, the Grand Duchy of Finland, had come into being. It was then that those institutions and, to a great extent, the buildings which still today house Finland's central administration were created. The President's office is of course in the former palace of the Czar.

The building up and the preservation of Finland's institutions and her special status was the oldest bureaucratic means of forming a national identity. With the exception of a Governor-General, the representative of the Czar, the Finnish civil service was composed entirely of native Finns. But it was only with the convening of the Diet that wider circles could make themselves felt. The Diet, which had assembled only once before, in Porvoo in 1809, was convened again in 1863 during Alexander II's period of liberalization, and from then on at regular intervals. With Europe experiencing a period of political reaction, Finland came under the severe and patriarchal rule of Czar Nicholas I. But Nicholas respected Finland's special status and during his reign a number of writers whose work went a long way to creating a sense of national unity in Finland emerged alongside the bureaucracy. J. L. Runeberg, Finland's national poet, in such works as *Elk Hunting on Skis* and *Tales of Ensign Stål* created an idealized picture of a poor but industrious Fininsh people living in harmony and contentment. These works contain an elevated but humane and often humorous description of the people, and includes what was to become the Finnish national anthem, »Maamme» (Our Land), in which the beauty of Finland's summer landscape becomes the

The 'national poet' J.L. Runeberg created an idealized image of the Finnish people and of the Finnish landscape: the summer panorama of an uninhabited land, evoking moral and religious associations. Runeberg's programme was consciously anti-revolutionary; he wrote his great nature poems between 1846 and 1853, a time of political unrest in Europe. Illustration by Edelfelt for Runeberg's *Tales of Ensign Stål.*

A romanticized view of Finnish literature: Finnish civilization is a national treasure, abandoned in the wilderness like the *kantele* in the picture. With the racial ideology that prevailed at the turn of the century, the idea of a Finno-Ugric or even a Turanian national identity gained currency in Finland, although the Finns' ties with the Hungarians and many tribes of central Russia are purely linguistic and, at that, mainly structural (similarities in vocabulary are limited, and those in cultural semantics non-existent).

object of love of the fatherland. Alongside the works of Runeberg, the body of Finnish folklore collected and presented in poetic form by Elias Lönnrot was to be of the greatest significance. This collection, the Finnish national Epic, the *Kalevala*, did much to spread an awareness of Finland's existence and special character throughout Europe in spite of the fact that, from the point of view of the emergent Finnish culture and even the Finnish language, the folklore on which it is based played a peripheral and receding role. It was not so much the contents or the language of the *Kalevala* which

The leading collector of ancient Finnish folk poetry was Elias Lönnrot, a physician and later professor of Finnish. He arranged the fragmentary original poems to produce the *Kalevala,* an epic poem modelled largely on Homeric precedent. Throughout Europe, the early 19th century was an era of grand, not always entirely authentic national epics.

Czar Alexander I doubled the funding of the University of Finland, which was transferred from Turku to Helsinki, the new capital of the Grand Duchy, and renamed the Alexander University. Behind the university building, a new age is dawning, and the muse, representing Finland, expresses the nation's gratitude to its ruler.

gave its publication such importance but the fact that Finns had been capable of such a cultural achievement. As distinct from Sweden, Finland had no history of its own, and (in a Romantic age, in which history, the Gothic and old ruins played an important role in the emergence of a national identity in many other countries) very few historical monuments. Thus Runeberg's »antique» concept of man and his idealization of the Finnish landscape together with the existence of the *Kalevala* were long to form the basis of a sense of Finnish national identity. It was only at the turn of the century that the *Kalevala*, as a source of inspiration to the masters of the »Golden Age» of Finnish art, was to have an important impact on Finnish culture.

The seal of Finland's oldest scientific academy, the Societas Scientiarum Fennica (Finnish Society of Sciences and Letters), founded in 1838.

Students drinking a toast in a Helsinki restaurant in the 1840s.

The fact that the country had only one University to train the entire future civil service was an important factor in bringing about Finnish unity. The University held a central position in the country's intellectual life since outside its circles cultural resourses were few. There were, after all, no large cities and no wealthy bourgeoisie, the nobility was small in number and the clergy was dispersed throughout the country. However, the University, which received the strong support of the government, did provide the prerequisites for literary and scienfic study and the organizations connected to the University were the only forums in which political debate was possible. Thus the University fulfilled an important function in training and supplying the human capital for the debate perios of the 1840's and for the critical years of the 1860's. A considerable proportion of the staff of the new Diet, of the journalists of the political and literary press and even of those people involved in creating a new era in art and industry were products of the University.

Along with the University, another important educational channel during Finland's period of autonomy was the Imperial Army. At the beginning of the 19th century one in five sons of the nobility, later one in nine, served in the Russian army, as did many outside the nobility, and Finland had its own Cadet School. The fact that about four hundred out of a total of some 3000 Finnish soldiers are known to have reached the rank of General or Admiral is a measure of their success. Many of these soldiers returned to Finland to take up posts in the civil service or to work in industry or other professions. Their period of service and the high-level training they received in different positions in the

The library of the Alexander University, designed by C. L. Engel and completed in 1844, is one of the finest works of architecture in Helsinki.

army of what was perhaps the most powerful state in the world brought the kind of insight and experience to Finland that did much to prevent the intellectual isolation which otherwise threatens a small country. The most well known figure to have chosen this path was the Finnish Field-Marshal, Mannerheim.

In spite of its autonomy Finland was not separated from Russia in other respects. Men from the local Russian garrisons were common sights in many Finnish towns. Along with them came Russian merchants and through their influence Orthodox churches were built. On the other hand there was a constant flow of people from eastern Finland to St. Petersburg where they either settled permanently or returned a few years later. The St. Petersburg economy, in other ways too, had a great influence on Finland.

The reign of Alexander II (1855–81), and in particular the 1860's, was a period of considerable liberalization in Finland, where reforms went on even after Russia itself had turned in a more conservative direction. The most important reform

Many Finns drew profit from the Russian Empire. The sons of Finland's small aristocracy served in the Imperial Army – as, indeed, did many other Finns – and, with their Lutheran morale and capacity for hard work, rose high in the ranks. One of the last of these was Baron Gustaf Mannerheim, who rose to Lieutenant-General in the Russian Army. The photograph shows him as a colonel and commander of the 13th Uhlan Regiment stationed in Poland. He later served as commander-in-chief of the Finnish Army in the Civil War of 1918, the Winter War in 1939–40 and the Continuation War in 1941–44. Regent of Finland in 1919 and President of the Republic from 1944 to 1946, he was awarded the title Marshal of Finland in 1942.

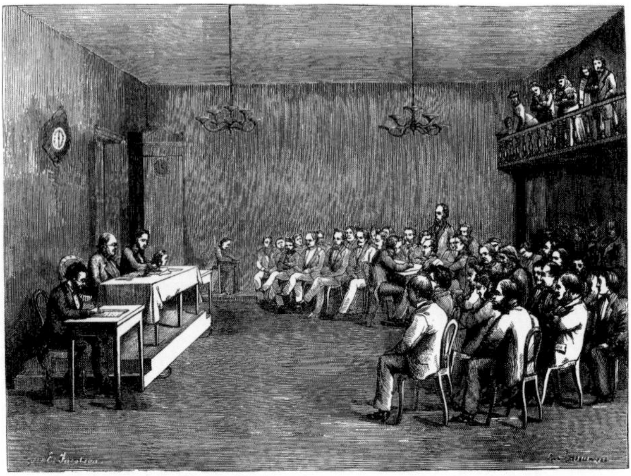

Russia and Poland did not have a parliament until 1906, but in Finland the Czar revived the old Diet of Estates. This body was convened regularly from 1863 on, and the Czar thus ruled Finland as a constitutional monarch. The picture shows a session of the commons; the nobility, clergy and burgesses convened in more sumptuous surroundings. Later on, fine buildings were erected in Helsinki to house the estates, but the unicameral legislature that resulted from the parliamentary reform of 1906 no longer had any use for them. When Finland achieved sovereignty in 1917–18, the only change made to the existing system was that the legislature was given parliamentary control over the executive branch, i.e. the government.

concerned the Diet. Following the convening of a preparatory committee in January 1861, the Diet of 1863–64 was held in Helsinki as were all subsequent ones. The rules of procedure for the Diet, which contained Four Estates until 1906, were enacted in 1869. Thus, at the beginning of the century, the bureaucratic society was being replaced by a civic society, one in which, it is true, the right to vote in matters of state was extended to only a very small section of the people, depending on the composition of the various Estates. The change-over to a new form of society was advanced by decrees granting self-administration to the provinces, uni-

A small steamship passing the Pälli locks of the Saimaa Canal. Passenger ships, wooden vessels known as 'tar steamers', and towed barges plied the canal.

versal freedom to ply a trade, permission to establish banks and limited companies, equal rights of inheritance to women and by the removal of education from the control of the Church, as well as a great many other reforms. From the 1860's onwards the establishment of numerous companies, societies and newspapers heralded the arrival of a new era.

The fact that new forms of livelihood were encouraged can be seen not only in the legislation of the time but also in policies regarding transport and communications. At the beginning of the 19th century, with the purchasing of coastal steamers and the building of canals, great strides were made in developing water traffic. The Saimaa Canal, an important Finnish waterway, was opened in 1856. Towards the end of the century an extensive network of railways was built, its main lines connecting Helsinki–Riihimäki–Wiborg–St. Petersburg, and with branch lines to Ostrobothnia (from Helsinki to Hämeenlinna as early as 1862), Savo, Karelia, Hanko and Turku. Internal migration, along with the transportation of goods, followed the direction of the railways. The »surplus population» of the inland areas of eastern Finland and Ostrobothnia moved to the rapidly growing city of Helsinki, to the industrial areas along the River Kymijoki, to the new port of Kotka, to Wiborg and Tampere, providing these areas with an industrial labour force. There was also a good deal of migration from eastern Finland to St. Petersburg and emigration to America, mostly from Ostrobothnia. For a long time to come industrial workers would be few compared to the number of those working in agriculture but the compact environment of the town facilitated the formation of workers' social and political associations – a typical feature of a newly industrializing and urbanizing

Tampere became Finland's leading industrial city. Here, a textile mill in Tampere in 1876.

society. Another feature typical of the times was the increasing importance of international trade and cultural exchange. The change-over to the metric system between the years 1887 and 1892 (a move which took place in Russia and Finland earlier than in many western European countries) can be seen as a sign of the significance of international commerce.

The fact that Finland had its own Diet, its own army and its own unit of currency, the Mark (it was

The old towns that dotted the Gulf of Bothnia coast transported inland goods to coastal regions and foreign countries. Tar barrels were a precious commodity in the

age of sailing ships. The fine church still dominates the skyline of Oulu, today a major industrial centre and the seat of a lively university founded in the 1950s.

introduced in 1860, released from its ties with the Ruble in 1865 and tied to the gold standard in 1878), had an important effect on the country's political and economic life and on the process of modernization, as well as having the greatest significance, both inside Finland and abroad, as symbols of the country's autonomy and internal self-government, particularly in view of the fact that Russia itself had no Parliament of its own and that the fiscal situation of the Russian Empire was less stable than that of Finland. As time went by the reforms brought about in Finland and the privileges gained there became the object of unfavourable attention

Finland's extensive territory was charted by means of scientific surveys, and many Finns participated in expeditions to various parts of Russia's vast reaches. The picture depicts the Sodankylä meteorological observation post in Finnish Lapland, 300 kilometres north of the Arctic Circle.

in Russia, especially because of their symbolic significance but also because of commercial competition. As the international political situation changed, Finland's position began to be more difficult. When, in 1871, Bismarck created a strong German state and relations between Germany and Russia later on grew more distant, Finland found itself in a sensitive strategic position. Criticism of Finland's political and economic autonomy and the country's links with the West, began to be expressed in Russia. However, the special status of Finland had the support of the ruler, and in 1878, during the Russo-Turkish War, own armed forces based on compulsory military service were even established for Finland.

During the early stages of Finland's autonomy it had been natural for Russia to support attempts to create a separate Finnish culture since this would serve to insulate the Finns from the Swedes. It would follow that, if Sweden tried to regain control of Finland, the Finns would not join the Swedes but would defend themselves and in so doing defend the Empire. During the Crimean War in the 1850's Sweden did in fact come close to allying itself to England and France who were active in the Baltic Sea and bombarding the coast of Finland. With the exception of a few liberal students the Finns demonstrated their solidarity with Russia in this situation. Nicholas I (whose reign is so often considered to have represented a period of reaction) had no reason, for example, to prevent the birth of the Society of Finnish Literature in 1831. It was during Nicholas' reign, in fact, that first a Finnish language lectureship (1828) and later a professorship (1850) were established at the University and this was at a time when new posts for lecturers in languages and

Like previous wars, the Crimean War in the 1850s was fought by Turkey and the western powers against Russia on two fronts, the Black Sea and the Baltic Sea. The allied British and French fleet devastated the Finnish coast, destroying virtually all of Finland's merchant fleet and bombarding Sveaborg and Helsinki. This picture shows the bombardment of Sveaborg. The Finns remained loyal to Russia.

particularly for professors were very rare indeed at universities anywhere. In the 1840's it began to be required that Finnish civil servants show proof of their command of the Finnish language and, in

1863, Czar Alexander II made Finnish an official language of administration and legal proceedings. In 1850, on the other hand, in order to prevent the circulation of political literature following the year of revolution in Europe (1848–49), the government placed a temporary restriction on publications in Finnish. The use of Finnish as a language of administration developed at the same time as the rise of a Finnish literary culture. Thus the press, on both languages, took on importance only in connection with the liberal breakthrough of the 1860's. The lack of intellectual resourses in Finland and not a conservative government policy, therefore, was the main obstacle to the growth of a Finnish-language

N° 1. THORSDAGEN,

SAIMA

1844. 4. JANUARI.

På denna Tidning, hvaraf ett nummer utgifves hvarje Thorsdag, prenumereras med Två Rubel Silfver, i Kuopio å Boktryckeriet, samt hos Kejserliga Postdirektionen i Helsingfors och å alla Postkontor med tillskott af vanligt postporto.

Hos Herrar Postförvaltare anhålles vördsammast att detta profnummer måtte utdelas till respektive prenumeranter på Finlands Allmänna Tidning.

UTNÄMND: Länebokh. i Vasa, Kronofogden Alex. Uggla, till Förvaltare af Kronomagasinet i Vasa.

VIGDE: Häradsh. Nils Michel Avellan och Demoiselle Sofia Lovisa Hackzell, i Åbo d. 24. Okt. — Justitie-Rådmannen P. Cederstein och Demoiselle M. S. Solin, i Raumo d. 10. Okt. — Handlanden C. J. Colliander och Demoiselle Angelique Pauline Berg, i Gamla Carleby d. 24. Juli. —

DÖDE: Länsmannen i Lappo socken, Exped. Fogden Johan Henric Tillman, d. 15. Nov. 62 år 2 m. 7 d. gammal. — Assess. och Stabsläkaren Carl Const. Frankenhaeuser's ömt älskade maka Sophia Berg, nära Viborg d. 8. Juli, i en ålder af 36 år. — Afl. Assess. Kr. Fogden och Riddaren Car. Eric Nordbergs enka Margaretha Clara Westzynthius, i Kemi d. 8. Nov., 82 år 4 m. 6 d. gammal. — v. Past. Erik Wahlbergs maka, Helena Sidensnöre, i Walkeala, 55 år gammal. — Amanda Emilia, dotter till Hof-Rätts Assessoren, Baron Carl Emil Lybecker och dess kära maka Lovise Agathe Krabbe, i Wiborg d. 3. Nov., nära 3 mån. gammal. — Handland. Matts Janell, i Brahestad d. 25. Okt., 77 år 8 m. 26 d. gammal. — Fendriks enkan, Helena Sofia Gren född Aländer, i Wiitasaari d. 15. Oct., 92 år g.

LEDIG TJENST: Läkare tjensten vid Finska Lifgardes Skarpskytte Bataljonen. — En Kommissions Landtmätare tjenst i Uleåborgs Län.

URARFVA ANSÖKNING: af afl. Kapellanen Gabr. And. Chydenii sterbhus delägare, inställelse dag efter natt och år från d. 4 Sept. inför H. R. i Pyhäjoki. —

CESSIONS ANSÖKNING: af Handl. Frans Wilh. Selin, hos R. R. i Vasa; inställelsedag: kl. före 12 på dagen första helgfria Måndag i Januari 1844.

FORDRINGSANSPRÅK: i Bonden Erik Andersson Välä Kuparis bo bör anmälas inför Borgå och Mäntsälä socknars H. R. andra rättegångsdagen af första lagtima Ting, som inträffar inom sex månader från d. 2. September 1843.

DOMAR: af R. R. i Lovisa uti Skepparen Elias Unonius Ch-sons konkurs d. 23. Dec. kl. 11 f. m.

ARFSANSPRÅK: Efter Peter Räsänens i Kaavi afl. hustru Margareta Karjalain, anmälas inom laga tid från d. 10 Nov. 1843.

TESTAMENTE: Organist-Enkan Maria Elisabeth Grundells till Guld och Silfver arbetaren M. Martins omyndiga barn samt Henr. Kraftmans omyndiga son Alandrus inför R. R. i Gamla Carleby.

ÄKTENSKAPSJAF: Mot Fredrika Sofia Lavander anmäles hos Pastors Emb. i Helsingfors inom 3 månader från den 25. Novemb. 1843.

OM TIDNINGAR I ALLMÄNHET OCH
Saima
I SYNNERHET.

I det skick, som för ögonen synes, får SAIMA äran framställa sig för den vördade allmänheten, önskande af allt hjerta, att samma vördade allmänhets anspråk måtte vara lika små som hennes egna. — Hon vågar hoppas detta i synnerhet på den grund, att hon sjelf framträder icke blott i skrift utan *tryckt* med goda corpus stilar. — Ty den enklaste erfarenhet skall vittna, att det med corpus tryckta omöjeligen kan hafva samma förmåga att fängsla uppmärksamheten som det skrifna. Skulle någon läsare betvifla sanningen häraf, så har han blott af nöden att betänka, hvad som borde skrifvas för en tidning, eller sjelf nedskrifva en artikel för denna, sådan den borde afhandlas. — och han skall lära inse, att det, som borde skrifvas, sällan tryckes, samt att det som tryckes aldrig tryckes såsom det kan skrifvas.

Hvilka än orsakerna härtill må vara, så neka likväl ingen, att ju Tidningar måste tryckas. Åtminstone kan om dem sägas, såsom Zigenaren sade om meneden: „hvartill skall väl mened finnas, om icke för att svärjas." Att de också böra läsas vill väl ingen blygsam Tidningsskrifvare påstå. — Men ett matt försök att läsa dem har dock sitt onekliga behag.
Och då så är, så följer häraf klarligen, att SAIMA har alldeles samma skäl för sitt uppträdande som landets öfriga Tidningar. Det är allt derföre som hon nu här niger för den vördade allmänheten — i synnerhet om vid det anförda besinnas, att ingen Tidning fås för intet. — Så är det också lätt afgjordt, hvad denna Tidning kommer att innehålla, nemligen: „just ingenting," och det vill säga: allt detsamma som träffas i andra Tidningar. För att i detta afseende vara desto säkrare, är SAIMA sinnad att ur dessa Tidningar låna så mycket som möjligt, med noga utsättande af hvilken redaktion för hvarje gång bragt detta intet i dagen — antingen såsom lån eller såsom egen uppfinning. — Man kunde anse för öfverflödigt att sålunda besitta just Ingenting *in dupplo*. Men medges måste, om eljest ännu 0 X 2 = 0, att genom detta fördubblande intet öfverflöd åstadkommits; och att SAIMA icke är öfverflödig kan således antagas vara mathematiskt, såsom en viss man plägar uttrycka sig.

Och dessutom kan SAIMA så godt som någon annan försäkra, att hon räknar sig till det — icke hemliga — sällskapet *utile dulci*, att hon skall gagna och roa, bjuda en på samma gång upplysande och underhållande läsning, att hon i synnerhet vill hålla sig till det fosterländska o. s. v. — ty hon vet, att den vördade allmänheten i all händelse icke tager hennes försäkringar för allvar, emedan den lika litet som hon på ett fremmande språk kan säga, hvad det fosterländska egentligen är, emedan den för öfrigt redan är upplyst och emedan blott kortspel är underhållande.

GYMNASIUM I KUOPIO.

Bland dagens nyheter är utan tvifvel underrättelsen, att Gymnasierna i Kuopio och Vasa redan nästa Augusti månad komma i verksamhet, den för landet mest betydelsefulla. Vi lemna derhän, huruvida formen af Gymnasium för en undervisningsanstalt är den lämpligaste, eller om den i Preussen och flera Tyska stater bestående inrättning, att Gymnasii- och Skol-undervisningen förenas i samma läroanstalt under *Skolans former*, borde föredragas. Ty det bättre är en fördel, äfven om det icke vore det bästa.

Också har underrättelsen om inrättandet af Gymnasium i Kuopio uti denna landsort väckt allmän glädje. För dess mottagande är allt snart förberedt. För detsamma står Högre Elementar-Skolans

The history of Finnish political journalism is considered to have begun with *Saima*, published by the noted philosopher J. V. Snellman, who later also published other newspapers. Snellman advocated broad participation by all strata of society (i.e., democracy), and therefore strove to improve the status of the Finnish language and education system. Nonetheless, Swedish remained the language of culture until the end of the 19th century; it was also the mother tongue of Snellman, Runeberg and other members of the elite. The Constitution Act of 1919 states that Finland's national languages are Finnish and Swedish.

culture. All in all the educated class was rather small which meant that it took a long time before they were able to create anything of a durable nature. This was true of both language groups. In Finland there were not, in fact, two distinct cultures, one Finnish-speaking and one Swedish-speaking: as far as output was concerned both cultures were essentially the same. The Finnish-speaking culture had long been dependent on the Swedish but, in terms of ideology, the Swedish-speaking culture was just as Finnish as the Finnish one itself. This ideology had been created by Runeberg, Lönnrot, Fredrik Cygnaeus, Snellman, Topelius and their contemporaries. Such figures as Yrjö-Koskinen and Julius Krohn (Suonio), who were responsible for much of the Finnish-speaking culture, had been brought up in Swedish-speaking and sometimes German-speaking environments. Many members of the educated class began quite voluntarily to use Finnish. The transition from one cultural language to another took place relatively slowly and smoothly. Generally speaking the question of language placed no national or social limits on the bilingual educated class. The bilingual tradition has been very strong in Finland and its culture, lasting at least until the second World War and is still, of course, very important today. This tradition has also kept Finland in close touch with the culture of Scandinavia. On the whole, the views on the position of the different languages were in close relation to the opinions about how desirable the participation of wide circles in social activities was.

The formation of interest groups into political parties, a process which had begun in the 1860's, was partly the result of disputes over the position of the languages. The national and social programme of the Fennoman Party, in particular (the party was led by Professor G. Z. Forsman, who wrote under the name of Yrjö Koskinen and was later elevated to the ranks of the nobility and given the title Baron Yrjö-Koskinen) was closely linked with demands for improvements in the position of the Finnish language, culture and economy. But, here too, what was involved was an entire programme which can be said to have represented, for the most part, the values and interests of the rural population, put forward in a spirit of national idealism and a kind of social conservatism. At this time the party was not an organization as such but consisted of a group of interests, supporting certain opinions, whose ranks included the majority of the clergy and the peasantry in the Diet, Finnish Clubs and Societies in many towns, almost the entire Finnish press, which was expanding rapidly at the time, and a good half of the student bodies, especially those representing the inland areas. In the 1890's the Fennoman Party was split into two when a nationalist-liberal faction of »Young Finns» with the daily newspaper *Päivälehti* (1889, *Helsingin Sanomat* since 1904) as its spearhead, set themselves in opposition to the »Old Finns» led by Yrjö-Koskinen and the newspaper *Uusi Suometar.*

The other party grouping comprised the majority of the nobility and the bourgeoisie in the Diet, student bodies representing the coastal areas, representatives of trade and industry and, in general, supporters of liberal ideas. This movement, whose most important supporter was the newspaper *Helsingfors Dagblad* (1862–89, said to be Finland's first modern newspaper) and of whose leaders the most well known was Leo Mechelin, later joined ranks with a group representing the Swedish-national

Until the early years of the 20th century, the Finns were a predominantly agrarian people. The urban population was small, and only really began to grow in the 1940s. Transport in the large but sparsely-populated country was based on waterways, doubling as ice routes in winter. Construction of an extensive rail network began in the 1860s, and was more or less completed by the turn of the century. The railways had a powerful centralizing impact on all spheres of activity.

ideal known as the »Viking Group», particularly after attempts by the liberals to form their own political party in 1880 had failed. Opposition to the language programme of the Fennoman Party was based largely on a desire to safeguard the standard of Finnish culture and out of concern for cultural links with the West and the basic precepts of constitutional politics. Swedish-language nationalism took on importance only when, following the Parliamentary reforms at the beginning of the 20th century, the appeal of the Swedish People's Party, founded in 1906, began to widen to include the rural Swedish-speaking population.

Under the rule of Alexander III (1881–1894) the special status of Finland was consolidated in many respects; this development was made possible by the strengthening of the Fennoman Party. The Fennoman Party had assumed an attitude of loyalty towards Russia and particularly the new ruler who at once adopted a semiparliamentary system by nominating as members of the Senate (or »ministers») leaders of parties of the Diet and, to an increasing extent, advocates of loyalty. The Fennoman senators pursued educational and agricultural matters.

During the latter half of the 19th century great changes occurred in rural conditions. An increase in the value of wood led, as a result of trade in timber, to a change from a subsistence agricultural economy to a monetary economy, widening the gap in the standard of living between those who owned forests and those who did not, with the latter losing their rights to the use of forest land. Rural conditions and the distribution of wealth were particularly affected by modernizations in agriculture – the development of methods of cultivation and cattle raising requiring greater capital outlay and producing larger profits. Cheap imported grain led to the domestic market concentrating on cattle farming and the exporting of butter. Farmers were able to increase their standard of living manyfold, renew their building stock, edu-

The Art Nouveau movement found inspiration in Finland's evergreen forests, snow-laden pine branches, cones, squirrels and bears. Woodcut by Akseli Gallen-Kallela (1899).

Gallen-Kallela, Jean Sibelius and Eino Leino infused their interpretations of the national epic, the *Kalevala* (1835, 1848), with an Art Nouveau spirit. Their imagery proved enduring. In this painting by Gallen-Kallela, the mother of Lemminkäinen, aided by a bee descending from heaven, is bringing her son back to life from the land of the dead, while the Swan of Tuonela glides past on the river of death. Sibelius composed a *Lemminkäinen Suite* in several movements.

Unveiling of the statue of Czar Alexander II in Helsinki's Senate Square, 1894. In front of the Czar stands the Maid of Finland, bearing a shield inscribed *Lex* and flanked by the Lion of Finland. The sculpture symbolizes Finland's privileged status within the Russian Empire, and has remained in place ever since it was unveiled.

ALEXANDER II

cate their children and purchase modern farming equipment, but only small changes were brought about in the conditions of the landless population and the difference between their standard of living and that of the landowners increased rapidly. The landless population comprised cottagers, who lived in rented cottages but had no land of their own,

With the development of icebreaker technology from the 1880s on, winter navigation gradually became increasingly practicable. The extent, thickness and formations of the Baltic ice cover vary considerably from year to year. This photograph dates from the winter of 1929.

hired farm-hands, who lived in and were dependent on the farm houses, as well as tenant farmers, who rented farm-land but were obliged to work for the landowners when he so required. A great many of the rural population (their numbers had grown considerably throughout the century) moved to the towns to work in industry or emigrated. It was the

Particularly in the 1860s, and up to the 1890s, crop failure and famine occurred repeatedly in Finland, as farming is always a risky business at these northern latitudes. This picture from the 1860s shows poor folk

being fed. Aggravated by the difficult transport conditions of the period, the famine took on disastrous proportions: one tenth of the Finnish people died of hunger or disease.

rural proletariat which suffered most during the years of crop-failures and particularly during the famine of 1867–68. There was an awareness that reforms were necessary to improve the conditions of the rural landless, but changes did not occur. In the first Parliamentary elections to embrace universal suffrage in 1907 it was the rural proletariat that guaranteed the enormous success of the radical Social Democratic Party. However, in the face of opposition from the Czar and the government, Parliament could not put reforms into effect, a situation which led to the social tension that was an important feature in Finland at the turn of the century.

Along with tension on the domestic front came increased tension between Finland and Russia. The growing power of the German state led to a military alliance between Russia and France at the beginning of the 1890's and the strategic importance of Finland's south coast became greater. While improvements in Finland's defence and system of railways were undertaken to meet the changing situation, greater and greater attention was being paid in Russia to the question of whether the Finnish people were still as loyal and trustworthy as they had been throughout the 19th century. In purely commercial terms Finland had already formed such strong ties with the West that her ties with Russia might be called into question, and strong cultural development was drawing Finland closer to Germany than to Russia. Russia made attempts to bring Finland more firmly back into its sphere of influence particularly in important military areas. But this led to conflict between the Russian government and the upper strata of Finnish society.

In 1898 the determined Russian General Nikolai Ivanovich Bobrikov became Governor-General of

Albert Edelfelt's celebrated portrait of
Pasteur reflects the fact
that prewar Finland belonged
to the general European cultural sphere.

Finland. The Manifesto of February, 1899, which was rather general in nature, represented his attempts to bring Finland back to the Russian fold. Faced with this situation, leading circles in Finland, particularly the alliance between the Swedish-minded Liberals and the »Young» Fennomen, which later formed the basis of the Constitutional of Opposition group, began to put up a concerted opposition. By making appeals to humanitarian and legal circles and by publicizing the achievements of Finnish culture and industry at such venues as the Paris World Fair in 1900, a great deal of attention was drawn to the Finnish question in Scandinavia, Germany and the western world in general. At home, public opinion was organized on a wider basis with the collection and presentation to the Czar of a »Grand Petition» signed by half a million Finns and especially by opposition to a law designed to conscript Finns into the Russian army. There were deep differences of opinion, however, as to what attitude should be taken to Russian aims. The »Old» Fennomen, in particular, favoured a strategy of negotiations aimed, primarily, at keeping the Senate and the administrative machinery in Finnish hands. The opposition, the Constitutionalists, saw this as following a line of submission. The »Old» Fennomen became embittered at doubts thrown on their patriotism for remaining in the Senate when their opponents resigned. Bobrikov's period, which is known emotionally as the »years of oppression», came to an end with his assassination in summer 1904 and to a political conclusion with the general strike of autumn 1905.

With Russia losing the war with Japan and the Czar obliged to agree to the establishment of a system of popular representation in Russia, the

Madame Paris welcoming little Mademoiselle Helsinki to the 1889 World Fair. The letters E.U. stand for *Exposition Universelle*. Finland emphasized its separate identity at these events, coming into conflict with Russia over the definition of this identity. At the 1900 World Fair, the Finnish pavilion and Finnish art attracted considerable political attention on account of the constitutional controversy which had just arisen between Russia and Finland at the time.

Radical political reform was carried out in Finland in 1906, when a joint decision of the Czar and the Diet of Estates set up a unicameral parliament and introduced universal suffrage. This also made Finland the first country to grant women both full voting rights and eligibility to public office. Here, a scene from the first electoral campaign in 1907. The Social Democrats gained a stunning 40 % of the vote. Socialist representation and women's suffrage were unusual enough in the world at the time, and were quite unprecedented in the Russian Empire, of which Finland was still a part.

government's policy towards Finland underwent a change. In Finland, the old Four-Estates Diet was replaced by a single-chamber Parliament in 1906. At a stroke Finland changed over from the oldest parliamentary system in Europe to the most modern. Under universal suffrage the number of voters in the country increased tenfold and Finland became the first country in Europe to extend the franchise to women. In the elections which followed, the Social Democratic Party, in which revolutionary views held an important position, gained 40 % of the mandate, its share increasing in subsequent elections until, in 1916, the socialists gained a majority in Parliament. The great reforms voted for in Parliament were not put into effect, however, as they were not ratified by the Czar and the Russian government.

Following the general strike and a shift in government policy in Russia, decrees enacted in Bobrikov's time were repealed and a Senate led by Mechelin came into power. Despite its reform, the new Parliament had no constitutional basis which meant that the Senate and the Governor-General were dependent on the confidence of the Czar. In 1909, as the political situation changed, first the Constitutionalists and later the »Old» Fennomen resigned from the Senate their place being taken by pro-government civil-servants who lacked the confidence of Parliament and the political parties, and from 1912 onwards, under a law giving equal status to Finnish and Russian subjects, by native Russians too. Finland's Governor-General from 1909 until the Revolution was General F. A. Seyn who was given the task of preventing the re-occurrence of such events as the general strike of 1905 and of thwarting Finnish and Russian revolutionary activities. This period of Finnish history is known as the second period of oppression but economically and culturally it was a fruitful time in many respects. It was also a time which saw, in addition to the growing tension in Finnish-Russian relations, a widening gap between bourgeois and socialist social groups. Under these conditions there was a growing desire, especially in Swedish-speaking quarters, to seek links with Sweden and, upon the outbreak of

Livestock farming became a vital source of livelihood for Finland during the latter half of the 19th century, as the construction of railways and better transport opportunities led to the replacement of domestic cereal crops with imported grain. Finnish butter became a major export article, much in demand on the Russian and British markets. As a source of independent income, dairy farming contributed to improving the status of women.

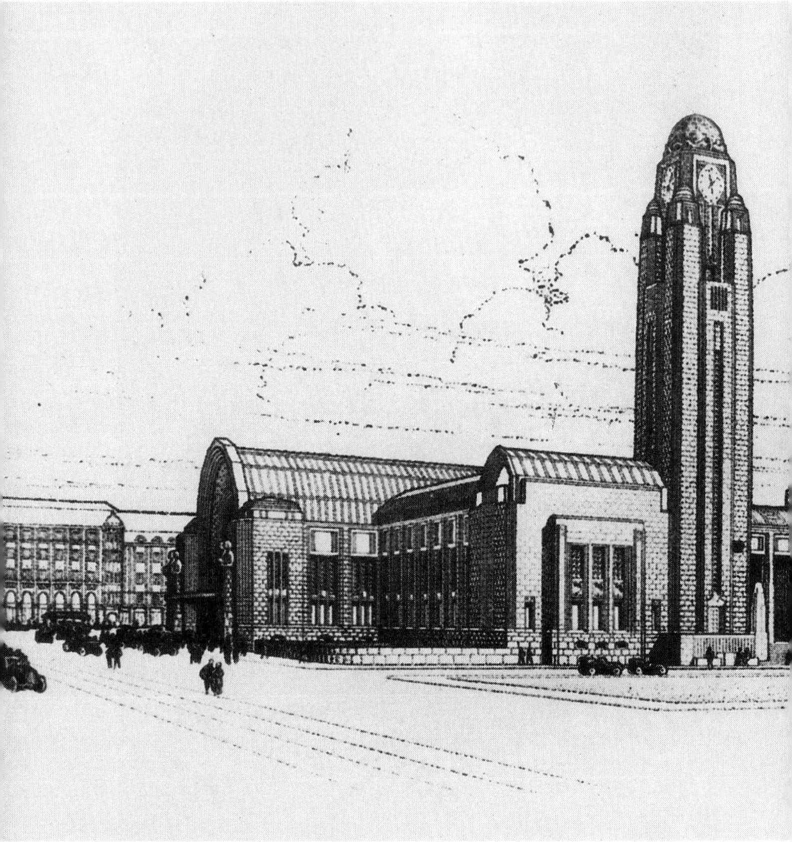

the first World War, with Germany. These aims are reflected in the fact that during the World War many young Finnish men volunteered to join not only the Russian army but also left to train as infantrymen in the army of the enemy, Germany, and that, following the war, White Finland (the country was divided into White and Red camps) formed close contacts with the still fairly strong Imperial Germany.

Helsinki Railway Station, completed in 1914,
shows how prosperous and advanced Finland had become
by the time. The Finnish railways still have
the Russian rail gauge. In the centre is the entrance to
the Imperial waiting room, used only once by Czar Nicholas II.
In later years, the entrance has been used for receiving
the heads of state of the Soviet Union and Russia.
Swedish, Danish and
Estonian state visitors have traditionally
arrived by sea; nowadays, of course,
they usually fly.

Czar Nicholas II in Helsinki during the First World War, when the Imperial Palace, today the President's Palace, served as a military hospital.

An obelisk topped by the two-headed Imperial eagle was erected in Helsinki's Market Square in honour of Empress Alexandra's first visit to Finland. The eagle was pulled down by Russian seamen in 1917, but was restored to its place in the 1960s.

Independent Finland

The Russian Revolution of March 1917 restored Finland to a position of autonomy. As the spring progressed, however, many Finns advanced the idea of complete independence from Russia while still more were of the opinion that Finland's future lay in the same kind of autonomous position that it had held under Russia in the 19th century. Those in favour of separation included, for the most part, the left-wing and the pro-German section of the bourgeoisie. In summer 1917, the Finnish Parliament, assumed the power that had been vested in the Czar, but the Russian Provisional Government under Alexander Kerenski, dissolved the Finnish Parliament and the enabling Act lapsed. These events widened the gap between the bourgeoisie and the left who had pushed through the Act. In the autumn elections the balance of power in Parliament changed with the bourgeoisie gaining a majority and Parliament decided once more to »assume authority» since attitudes towards Russia in bourgeois circles had been changed once and for all by the October Revolution. The so-called Independence Senate, led by P. E. Svinhufvud proposed to Parliament that Finland should declare independence and that the new sovereign state should be a Republic. The proposal was approved by Parliament on December 6th, 1917. Foreign powers were unwilling to recognize Finnish independence before the Soviet government had done so. On 31st December, 1917, upon the request of the Senate, Lenin's government announced its recognition of the new state, after which France, Sweden, Germany, Austro-Hungary, Greece, Norway and Denmark quickly followed suit; Great Britain and the United States, on the other hand, recognized Finland's independence only one and a half years later. Rec-

Lenin's Soviet Russia recognized Finland's sovereignty on January 4, 1918. Sweden, Germany and France rapidly followed suit, as indeed did most countries of Europe. Britain and the United States recognized Finland's independence only over a year later, as they considered that Finland had changed sides and come under the sphere of influence of the German Empire, which was in fact true. The first of the new states to be born in the wake of the First World War, Finland already had a political identity, although not as a sovereign state. In this caricature, Lenin, assisted by the King of Sweden and the German Kaiser, places the French cap of freedom on the Maid of Finland's head.

ognition of Finnish independence, however, did not mean the withdrawal of Soviet troops stationed in Finland in spite of attempts by the Finnish Senate to accomplish this.

The socialists were no longer so eager to break with Russia. The radical left, hoping for a revolution in Finland too, achieved the ascendancy in the Social Democratic Party. At the end of January, 1918 the »Reds» took over power in Helsinki and southern Finland. The Senate fled to Vaasa in Ostrobothnia where they established a »White» stronghold controlling northern and central Finland. General Gustaf Mannerheim was called in to take control as commander-in-chief of the »White» forces and, at the beginning of April he won the decisive battle for Tampere. At the same time, at the invitation of the Senate, a German division landed on the south coast of Finland, taking Helsinki and other towns. The role played by the Germans in supporting the »Whites» and that of Russia in supplying arms and assistance to the »Reds» is a clear indication of the fact that, in addition to Finland's internal affairs, the war also involved the question of the spheres of interest of the Major Powers. At the outbreak of the first World War Germany had already attempted to pave the way to rebellion in Finland by training a group of Finnish volunteers as light-infantrymen. With the end of the war in spring 1918, Germany made efforts to tie Finland firmly to its sphere of interest. At the political level this is seen from the fact that the Kaiser's brother-in-law, Prince Friedrich Karl of Hessen, was elected King of Finland. Germany's collapse prevented him from ever ascending the throne, however, and at the same time Finland was freed from its economic and military alliance with

Jean Sibelius produced his major compositions during the first quarter of the 20th century, and was already famous before the First World War. His musical idiom progressed from Art Nouveau romanticism to classicism, combining rustic (Finnish) and cultivated (Swedish) elements with Russian and German impulses into a unique musical language. Sibelius's worldwide reputation was of comparable significance to Finland as that of the *Kalevala* in the previous century; together with Mannerheim, he is the most famous Finn of all time. Drawing from 1908 by Sibelius's brother-in-law Eero Järnefelt.

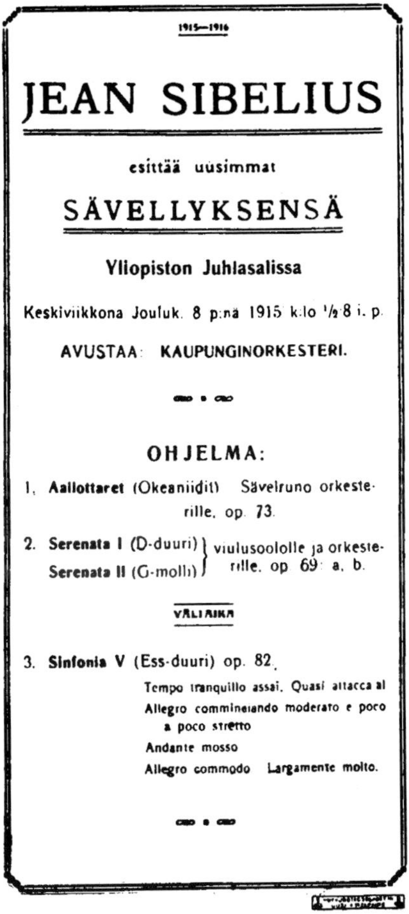

1915—1916

JEAN SIBELIUS

esittää uusimmat

SÄVELLYKSENSÄ

Yliopiston Juhlasalissa

Keskiviikkona Jouluk. 8 p:nä 1915 k:lo ½8 i. p.

AVUSTAA: KAUPUNGINORKESTERI.

OHJELMA:

1. **Aallottaret** (Okeaniidit) Sävelruno orkesterille, op. 73.

2. **Serenata I** (D-duuri) / **Serenata II** (G-molli) } viulusoololle ja orkesterille, op. 69: a. b.

VÄLIAIKA

3. **Sinfonia V** (Ess-duuri) op. 82.
   Tempo tranquillo assai. Quasi attacca al
   Allegro commineiando moderato e poco a poco stretto
   Andante mosso
   Allegro commodo Largamente molto.

Sibelius gave a performance of his »most recent works», including the Fifth Symphony, on his 50th birthday, December 8, 1915. The war had not directly affected Finland yet, although many Russian troops were stationed in Finland to forestall a possible German invasion. The war arrived in Finland with a vengeance in spring 1918, when the 'Whites' and 'Reds' fought a bloody civil war in which German and Russian troops were also involved.

Germany. Mannerheim, who had opposed the pro-German trend in Finland, became regent and under his leadership the country began to look towards the western world. On 17th July, 1919 the Constitution, which is still in force, was ratified by Mannerheim and Finland's relations with foreign states were normalized. Under a peace treaty signed with Russia at Tartu (Dorpat) in 1920, the area of Petsamo in Lapland was added to Finland's former territory, which meant that the country now extended to the Arctic Ocean; Finland was later to lose this area under the armistice of 1944.

The Finnish Constitution was created as a compromise between republican and monarchist opinion. It left the President with most of the power enjoyed by the head of state under the previous constitution: responsibility for foreign policy, the position of Commander in Chief of the army and the right to dissolve Parliament. While the President's position within the system of state became of central importance, a multi-party system led to short-term governments varying in their political composition.

With the Constitution affording the President a central position in affairs of state, the first two Presidents of the Republic, K. J. Ståhlberg and L. Kr. Relander, both exercised their right to dissolve Parliament in the face of opposition from the Council of State. Neither did the next President, P. E. Svinhufvud adhere to the classical principles of democracy, with minority governments in power through most of his term of office. By contrast K. Kallio's term of office was a period of government by broadly-based coalitions. Under R. Ryti, Finland's war-time President, and the five post-war Presidents, G. Mannerheim, J. K. Paasikivi, U. K.

Kekkonen, M. Koivisto and Martti Ahtisaari, the President's position as leader of the country's foreign policy has taken on an ever greater importance, a development which has naturally also affected Finland's internal affairs. While the President's position has been thrown into relief by the short duration of the various governments, the fact that the same individuals have held ministerial positions in successive governments has made for a certain continuity. Parliamentary elections have for a long time been fairly stable; the 1930's saw a growth in support for the Right, with a corresponding increase in support for the Left in the years immediately following the war. With the exception of Tanner's minority Social Democratic government (1926–1927) the 1920's was a period of government by centre and centre-right coalitions. The 1930's was a time of »Pre-sidential» governments (foremost among which was the long-lived Kivimäki administration) until 1937 when, with K. Kallio becoming President, a Social Democrat–Agrarian–Progressive Party coalition came into power.

The greatest change to take place in the form of government since independence, apart from the change-over from a heriditary monarchy to a regularly elected head of state, was the adoption of Parliamentary principles. Otherwise Finland, unlike most other countries achieving independence after World War I, already had its own system of representation and administration, elections by universal suffrage, its own civil service and financial institution, its own economy and culture.

The political significance of the war of 1918 lies in the fact that it determined whether Finland would follow Russia on the road to revolution. In

The rivers of northern Finland and the lakes of the interior were log-floating highways for many decades. The timber was floated

hundreds of kilometres to the sawmills and pulp and paper mills on the coast. The river in the photo is the Kemijoki.

the anti-revolutionary sense, in removing Russian troops from Finland and securing the country's political independence, it was a »war of liberation» which came to a conclusion at Tarto in 1920. As a »civil war» its roots lay largely in the growing dissatisfaction with social inequalities that had long been smouldering beneath the surface. Soon after the war the reforms which had long been planned but which had been postponed because of political circumstances, were put into effect. The most important reform concerned the finding of land for the landless population and freeholds for tenant farmers.

During the early years of independence acts were passed introducing compulsory education, prohibition of alcohol (repealed in 1932), freedom of worship, freedom of speech and freedom to form societies. Legislation was introduced regulating the position of the two language groups and an Act was passed providing autonomy for the Åland Islands, an area over which Finnish sovereignty had been confirmed by the League of Nations and which had long represented a bone of contention between Finland and Sweden. During Ståhlberg's period as President, an Act of Amnesty was passed under which those convicted as leaders of the »Reds» were quickly pardoned in an attempt to dispel the destructive memories of the War in 1918. In the spring of 1919, the Social Democratic Party, the representative of the losing side in the war, could participate in the elections and became the largest party in Parliament. As early as 1926 the Social Democrats alone formed the Government, a fact which can be seen as an indication of the stabilization of the democratic system. This success is explained in part by the fact that the Left had split in two, with the Social Democrats representing the moderate wing of the old Socialist Party. The revolutionary wing founded the Finnish Communist Party in the Soviet Union in 1918, but this was illegal in Finland until 1944. Otherwise the Agrarian Party and the Swedish Party continued as before with the Finnish-speaking section of the bourgeoisie re-forming their ranks to fight over the constitutional form the country was to have. The monarchists formed the National Coalition Party which was made up for the most part of members of the »Old» Fennoman Party, while the Republicans formed the Progressive Party around a core of »Young» Fennomen. In addition to two other small parties, the Christian Party and a political group which fronted for the Communists, another party to emerge at this time was the Fascist-like Patriotic People's Movement (IKL). Founded in 1933, its early support soon dwindled and it was proscribed under the armistice of 1944.

In spite of many economic difficulties and a relatively low standard of living, a spirit of optimism prevailed in Finland throughout the 1920's, a mood which was heightened by the success of Finnish sportsmen, by the apperance of new literature, by the kind of international intercourse, with its diplomats and state visits, for which sovereignity is a prerequisite, and by Finland's participation in the League of Nations. On the other hand, the world-wide economic depression at the end of the decade led to difficulties in Finland too: bankruptcies, auctions of property and shortages. The language disputes, which had flared up once again, were a prominent issue throughout the 1920's and 1930's, but they did not lead to any legislation of note.

The great depression, which began at the end of the 1920's and continued until the middle of the next decade, was felt in Finland too, both financially and politically. Unemployment grew and in an agrarian country the fact that on a large scale smallholdings had such debts that they were forced to compulsory auctions was a disturbing phenomenon. Many banks were obliged to stop functioning or to merge with larger banks.

The social crisis naturally increased political pressures. Linked to this was the worry concerning the spread of communism and the developments within the Soviet Union. The collectivization and the population transfers in the Soviet Union gave visible reason to fear changes. It was under such circumstances that the anti-communist Lapua movement was born and grew. The movement which gained wide support in 1930 at the time of the great peasants' march to Helsinki gradually became more radical culminating in an attempt at an armed rebellion in spring 1932. The movement was part of a general European trend against liberalism and the parliamentarism of the 1920's: in place of the monetary power, moral degeneration which they represented, more state control and planning were sought particularly so that new attempts at the failed leftist revolutions after the world war could be prevented. Although there had been a left wing revolution in Finland in 1918, Finland preserved a parliamentary model throughout the 1932 situation and its after effects. This soon drew Finland closer to the other Nordic countries particularly since the Baltic countries and especially Germany were moving in the 1930's to a one-party system and dictatorial power.

After 1932 in Finland too there was a movement

to long-term governments. At first the government was weak as far as parliamentary support was concerned and it leant above all on the President (P. E. Svinhufvud). It stabilized the situation both politically and financially and began to move the emphasis of foreign policy away from the League of Nations towards the security system of the Nordic countries. In 1937, with a change in Presidents, the so-called »red-green» coalition was formed, in which the Agrarian Party and the Social Democrats began a long period of co-operation. As far as internal politics were concerned it meant the rejection of the 1918 division, agreement over the language disputes of the 1920's and 1930's, and the beginning of a social security system: as far as foreign policy was concerned it meant co-operation with the Swedish Social Democrat government and the rejection of the German alternative. The Foreign Ministers were Anglophiles, the government coalition resembled slightly the French example, and the general direction was towards the Nordic countries. Financial development and a rise in the standard of living also muffled the extreme right wing, and the fascist-like IKL Party which was born out of the Lapua movement was reduced to a minor factor.

The general liberalizing tone of the thirties was expressed in the Anglosaxon tone of the newspapers and films, whereas the stimulus for the pictorial arts and architecture came mostly from France. In place of Neo-Classicism came the Functionalist style with its predominance in building production, metal furniture and the Artek form based on the use of Finnish materials. In the field of philosophy and the »world view» logical empirism and the new trends in psychology, particularly freudism, received wide attention; the general trend in cultural life changed from the narrowly nationalistic to a more open attitude to Europe, and in the field of the natural sciences the influence of the United States began to be felt at the end of the decade.

In this optimistic atmosphere the threat of a great war did not lead to any considerable development in defensive preparedness in spite of the reports of Marshal Mannerheim, who had become chairman of the Defence Council at the beginning of the decade. When, therefore, the Soviet Union as early as 1938 secretly and in 1939 publicly demanded negotiations and exchanges of territory, Finland did not for a long time believe that the demands would lead to war. The Soviet Union's attack in November 1939 was to Finland and the world to a great extent a surprise.

The Soviet Union had that classic security problem: the need to shift the defence of Leningrad and north-west Russia back to the mouth of the Gulf of Finland, since on Finland's and Estonia's independence it had been obliged to draw the line very close to Leningrad. Estonia and the other Baltic countries did provide the Soviet Union with bases in autumn 1939; Finland was prepared to discuss changes of territory on the Karelian Isthmus, but did not feel it was possible to negotiate about a base on the Hanko peninsula.

Also the situation that had come about when the Soviet Union and Germany had entered into an alliance and had made a secret division of interests was for Finland quite new. Germany did remain neutral during the Winter War, according to agreement. Neither did Finland's hopes to realize a Nordic Country defence plan come about: the country was obliged to go to war alone and ill-equipped.

The Soviet Union attacked Finland on November 30, 1939, expecting a rapid victory. Hitler and Stalin had just allotted Finland to the Soviet sphere of influence in their pact. Finland held on, however, during three months of extreme cold, destroying whole Russian regiments, which were unaccustomed to winter warfare, and generating an unprecedented national solidarity and defensive will. As there were no other war operations going on at the time, the attention of the international press focused on Finland, which gained a great deal of goodwill as a result of the *Winter War*. On March 13, 1940, Finland, still unoccupied, made an honourable peace (though its terms were harsh), and preserved its independence.

But the Soviets too had difficulties and inexperience particularly in respect of winter warfare, and the Finnish army – whose Commander in Chief had become Marshal Mannerheim – achieved several considerable victories in repelling attacks to begin with in the north, at Suomussalmi and Raate where the Red Army tried to push their way towards Oulu in order to cut Finland in two. It was, however, clear that Finland could not last long against an enemy of far greater power. When the Soviet Union gave up its support to the marionette government it had established on the Karelian Isthmus, an armistice was concluded in March 1940. The Finnish army had withdrawn and was forced to surrender Viipuri (Vyborg) but the front held out until the end and partly guaranteed the preconditions for an honourable but heavy defeat. It realized the Soviet Union's original aims: a base in Hanko and the moving of the border further from Leningrad.

The area surrendered was about one tenth of Finland's area and the population slightly more: all Karelians thought it better to come to what was left of Finland than to remain in their home districts. In terms of those fallen and wounded Finland's losses in the Winter War had been great. The Winter War left the Finns with a feeling of injustice which was mitigated by the awareness that the result, the maintenance of sovereignty, was gained by unanimity and resolution. These factors had an important effect in reorientation when relationships between the Soviet Union and Germany began to be strained. Germany began to show an interest in Finland and this was received in post-war Finland with a sense of relief, in a situation in which Soviet politics were understood in wide circles to be still anti-Finland. When Hitler attacked the Soviet Union in the summer of 1941 there were already German troops in northern Finland which in fact became an area of German military operations. The situation in Northern Europe had undergone a drastic change by the incorporation of the Baltic Countries into the Soviet Union and the occupation of Denmark and Norway by Germany. German operations in northern Finland related, as a matter of fact, to Norway.

Finland did not, however, form an alliance with Germany and both the Finnish government and the Commander in Chief followed strategy which served the purposes of Finland alone during the war. Thus Finland did not actively participate in the siege of Leningrad nor did it break Leningrad's service line to the Arctic Ocean. Mannerheim understood that Finland and the Soviet Union or Russia would still be neighbours even after the war. Finland did, however, occupy part of Eastern Karelia on the

The war years resulted in the large-scale evacuation of territories ceded to the Soviet Union. Sweden donated large amounts of humanitarian aid to Finland, and received children, war invalids and evacuees from Finland. All the inhabitants of the ceded territories – about one tenth of the overall population – were resettled in other parts of Finland.

As far as Finland was concerned, the enemy was the same in 1939 and 1943, although some of those who identified with the Allies took Stalin's side. Cartoon by Tove Jansson, 1943.

other side of the border. There were plans to annex this area to Finland. This was the area that Finland had tried to obtain in 1919–1920 and in 1939 the Soviet Union had offered this area to Finland as an exchange of territory and also annexed it to Finland with an agreement made that year by the marionette government. Essentially, however, it was a question of moving the war into the adversary's territory, of a tactical viewpoint and a potential territory for exchange during the making of peace.

From the year 1943 onwards Finland investigated the possibility of a separate peace but, on the one hand, the situation concerning supplies and the fear of a German occupation and, on the other hand, the harsh peace terms postponed the armistice until September 1944. In the spring 1944 there had been heavy bombing of particularly Helsinki and, during summer, extremely severe fighting on the Karelian Isthmus where the advance of enemy had been halted, on the one hand, at Vuoksi in the fierce battles of Taipale and, on the other hand, west of Vyborg in the heavy battles of Tienhaara, Tali and Ihantala. At this point Finland made a pact with Germany and received significant armament aid, especially for air warfare, but denounced the pact already two months later, when paving the way for a peace treaty. The first step consisted in a change of president whereby Finland simultaneously freed itself from its commitments to Germany. Elected President of Finland in early August 1944 was the Commander in Chief Mannerheim who had been nominated Marshal of Finland on the 75th celebration of his birthday in 1942.

The 1944 truce which was ratified at the Paris Peace Congress of 1947, returned the borders to the situation in 1940 in Karelia; instead of Hanko the peninsula of Porkkala was now rented to the Soviets for 50 years, and the vast area of Petsamo acquired in 1920 was lost. Finland had to expel the Germans from Lapland which took several months and caused great devastation. It also had to agree to pay heavy war reparations and accept certain restrictions concerning the size of its army, etc. But the country retained its sovereignty and the Control Committee set up by the allies left the country

The armistice of 1944 was ratified by Finland and the Allied Powers in the Paris Peace Treaty of 1947. Finland was obliged to undertake enormous war reparations, which were paid in kind. Finland was the only country to pay its reparations in full; the photograph shows the last trainload of goods, which crossed the border in September 1952. The industrial sectors developed in order to pay the reparations later continued to produce goods for conventional export to the Soviet Union; meanwhile, Finland's now ultra-modern industry was also able to gain a foothold on Western markets.

619

immediately after the Paris Peace Treaty. The payment of reparations in full in 1952 and the Soviet Union's relinguishment of the Porkkala base in 1955 removed the last restrictions to sovereignty.

The 1941–44 war is known in Finland as the »continuation war» because it was understood as an extension of the Winter War and as an attempt to compensate for losses suffered in that war. The history behind the Winter War explains why Finland participated in the war alongside Germany: in the great power competition between Germany and the Soviet Union/Russia, Finland could not have chosen the side of the Soviet Union in 1941. It was obliged to choose one side or the other for reasons of supplies and in order to avoid a possible occupation like that of Norway and Denmark. But Finnish state leaders and military leaders stressed consistently and with success the special character of Finland and its independence in the war. In Finland there was only very marginal interest in the ideology of national socialism, and the Finnish government refused all ideological co-operation with Germany and, for example, rejected entirely any proposed measures against Finland's jews. These factors made it possible to withdraw from the war a year before Germany's collapse and to turn their weapons against their former brothers in arms. But of course the change in direction was psychologically demanding particularly since fears concerning the aims of the Soviet Union were deep; the authority of Marshal Mannerheim, the President-Commander in Chief, in accepting peace and beginning war against the Germans in Lapland was decisive.

Finland felt its situation poor, difficult and threatened, relative to the Soviet Union, which had become a great power and Sweden, which had

The Russians leaving the Porkkala base near Helsinki, leased by them for 50 years under the truce agreement. Besides international *détente* and Russia's wish to exert pressure on its adversaries to do likewise, the Russian decision to give up the base reflected Finland's success in establishing good working relations with its large and unpredictable eastern neighbour.

avoided the war and become wealthy during it, the Baltic countries, which had lost their independence and Germany, which had become an economic and political void. In the continuation war Finland's number of fallen was 65 000 and of wounded 158 000, homes had to be found for over 423 000 Karelians (representing 11 % of Finland's population), jobs had to be found for those returning from war and the war reparations, which placed Finnish production under extreme conditions, had to paid. The demands of the victors, the Soviet Union and Great Britain, to condemn the war guilty, that is to say the political leaders during the war, had a great psychological effect on the country. The war trials led to the conviction of the wartime President Ryti, two former Prime Ministers and some other political leaders to prison sentences of different lengths, at most ten years. However, compared to other countries which had participated in the war, Finland suffered relatively lightly. Above all this was due to the fact that neither side had occupied Finland; Finland's defence during the summer of 1944 would have made the occupation of the country too costly for the Soviet Union. Neither did Germany have adequate power to bend Finland, which had changed sides, to its will. Popular humour soon found expression, now a classic, for the result of the war: the Soviet Union won but Finland came second.

As a consequence of the war Finland went through a fast and at the beginning difficult economic and social change, and it took a long time before the level of pre-war production and standard of living were reached and passed. Such was the situation also in other countries that had gone to war, although in Finland as a neighbour of the well-off Sweden, this was soon forgotten. But the period of change took place organizationally without radical changes in the social system. Finland's constitution of 1919 remained in force, and the government leant the whole while on a parliament elected by free elections. The highest decision-making power represented long traditions: the President-Commander in Chief Mannerheim, the Prime Minister and future President J. K. Paasikivi (elected to office in 1946) and the post-war Foreign Minister Carl Enckell had all been in leading political positions ever since Finland had become independent and they all knew Russia well even though they were not experts in communist ideology. Among the younger politicians Urho Kekkonen of the Agrarian Party and K. A. Fagerholm of the Social Democrats, both of whom had been Prime Ministers during the Paasikivi period, had both been members of parliament and ministers as early as the 1930's, Fagerholm even in the war cabinet. In addition to the Agrarian Party and the Social Democrats, the People's Democrats led by the communists were in the government 1945–48. The communist participation in the government had a remarkable effect on the stabilizing of internal politics in the immediate post-war years. The changeover in power in Czechoslovakia in spring 1948 also led to a change of government in Finland. Paasikivi formed a Social Democratic minority government led by Fagerholm even though this did not please the Soviet Union. The People's Democrats returned to government only in the 60's.

In its foreign policy Finland gave most importance to cementing good relations with the Soviet Union even though this led to many difficult situations as the Cold War deepened. Thus Finland

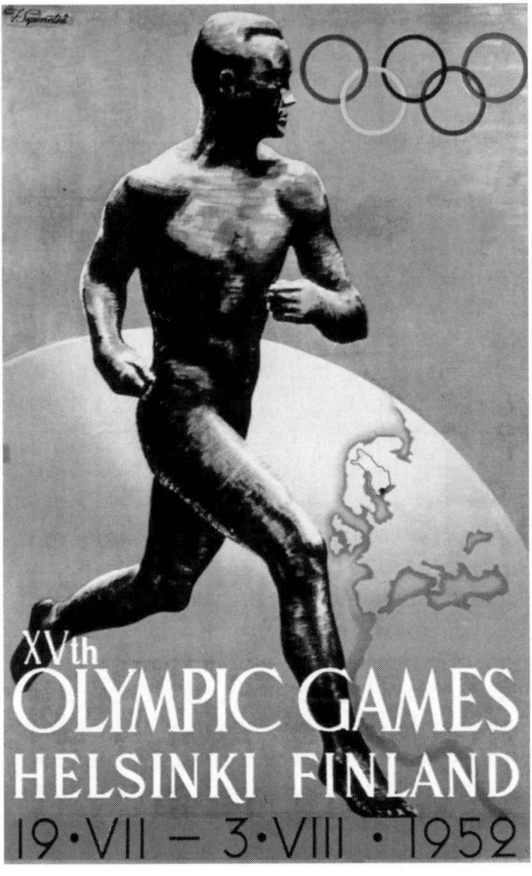

Helsinki had been promised the 1940 Olympic Games, but they were cancelled on account of the Second World War. The 1952 Olympics were held in Finland even though the country had fought on the losing side in the war. The Games gave a tremendous boost to the nation's self-respect, and showed the rest of the world that Finland had survived the war and the postwar years as a Western democracy and a nation that had preserved its honour. The figure on the poster is the renowned Finnish long-distance runner Paavo Nurmi.

refused Marshall aid because of the political ties which this implied, but Finland did receive considerable loans from the United States which significantly helped in stabilizing the economic situation in the country. The payment of war reparations were carried out precisely and on schedule even though it put the national economy and industry under great strain. On the other hand this forced the country to restructure its industry which soon began to pay off. The loans received from the United States and Sweden were mostly used to modernize industry and develop exports.

From the military policy viewpoint the Finnish position was restricted by the conditions contained in the truce of 1944 and the Paris Peace Treaty of 1947 concerning the Finnish defence forces and the number of its weapons, conditions which the allies later mitigated. As early as 1945 Marshal Mannerheim stressed to the Soviet Union that it was also within Soviet interests that Finland had efficient defence forces. This led to the 1948 Treaty of Friendship, Co-operation and Mutual Assistance with the Soviet Union in which Finland agreed to prevent any attack on the Soviet Union through Finnish territory. This treaty remained in effect until 1991. The treaty worked as intended and freed the Soviet Union from the classical worry over the security of Leningrad, but there was never any need to put into operation the article concerning consultations on the threat of attack through Finnish territory. The treaty was therefore a kind of declaration in principle. The Finnish aim to remain outside conflicts between the great powers was mentioned at the beginning of this treaty.

The stabilizing influence of Finland's relations with the Soviet Union was felt in wider circles around the Baltic Sea during the era of Soviet might from the World War until the disintegration of the Union of Soviet Socialist Republics in 1991; from at least the beginning of the 1960's also all the western powers repeatedly recognized the success of Finland's policy of neutrality. Even so, the position of Finland as a good but nevertheless non-socialist neighbour to the Soviet Union was sometimes difficult to perceive both in Finland and the Western countries; when international tension decreased, the position of Finland was admired, during periods of strained relations between the great powers there were doubts about Finnish independence and credibility abroad – not on the part of governments but frequently indeed on that of the press, often on the basis of private Finnish or even more often Swedish views. Every now and then it thereby remained unnoticed that the relationship between Finland and the Soviet Union was built upon the basic geographic factors of the Baltic Sea and the Gulf of Finland region. Soviet security interests and Finland's desire not to become an arena for a conflict between the great powers – to prevent the recurrence of the situation which led to the wars of 1939 and 1941 – remained permanent at least as long as the Union of Soviet Socialist Republics existed and were fundamentally conveyed to the relationship between Finland and Russia. These military and political viewpoints were in a most essential respect for decades supported by mutual economic interests.

Finland also initiated economic co-operation with the Soviet Union after the war and from 1952 onwards a great share of the products of the war reparation industry became export articles to the Soviet Union.

The period after the war, particularly the period which started in 1952 after the payment of war reparations, resembled the situation at the turn of the century. The Soviet Union's large markets and the Finnish structure of production fit each other well. About 15 to 25 % of Finnish exports went to the Soviet Union and for long periods Finland was the Soviet Union's greatest non-socialist trading partner after West Germany. The main import from the Soviet Union was energy; natural gas, nuclear power and above all oil, whereas Finland exported consumer goods such as clothes, shoes and furniture as well as machines and most visibly shipping, ice-breakers and large construction projects, in which the Finns planned and built in the areas of Leningrad, Karelia and Estonia, not only hospitals and hotels but also large harbours and entire industrial towns.

The changeover from barter to foreign exchange trading made the Finnish Eastern Trade collapse in 1990 and it was not until 1993 that trade began to slowly recover, but now it was entirely new in structure.

Entering into the great volume of Soviet trade and embarking on long term projects meant a great change in the structure of production immediately after the war. The war reparations demanded by the Soviet Union had to be paid in the form of products defined by the victor and this forced Finland to speed up its process of industrialization. Commerce between Finland and the Soviet Union made the relationship between the two countries more practical and concrete. Trade thus removed prejudices and those psychological constraints which were brought about by the experiences of war, by the difference in language and culture, and by the

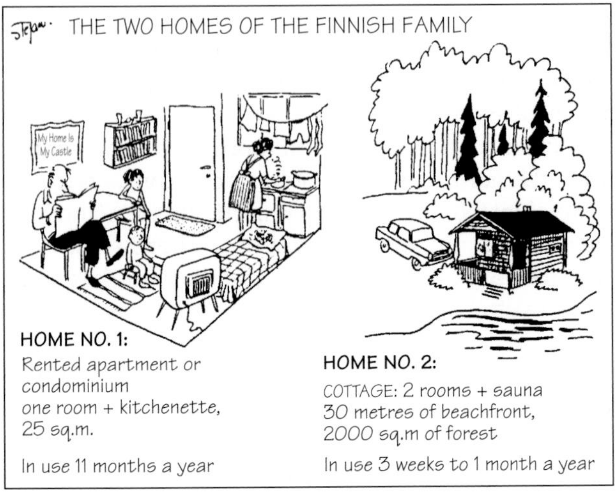
THE TWO HOMES OF THE FINNISH FAMILY
My Home Is My Castle
HOME NO. 1:
Rented apartment or condominium
one room + kitchenette,
25 sq.m.
In use 11 months a year
HOME NO. 2:
COTTAGE: 2 rooms + sauna
30 metres of beachfront,
2000 sq.m of forest
In use 3 weeks to 1 month a year

An integral element of the Finnish identity in the postwar period was holiday living, as virtually every family acquired a summer cottage of its own. This phenomenon reflected the country's very recent urbanization, which had given the people only a thin urban veneer. Gradually mass tourism to the Mediterranean region began to compete with and replace cottage holidays. The cartoon, with the caption »The Two Homes of the Finnish Family», juxtaposes the close quarters to which Finns are confined in the winter with the profusion of space available during the summer season.

differences between socialist societies and market economy democracies. In addition there was still the difference in size between a world power and a small state – in St. Petersburg alone there are about the same amount of people as in the whole of Finland. It was of mutual interest to both countries to show that peaceful coexistence between countries of different social systems could function well. Finnish foreign policy led to the fact that at the end of the sixties and during the seventies Helsinki was accepted as neutral territory for important international negotiations in addition to the classical Vienna and Geneva.

Another cornerstone of Finnish post-war politics was the strengthening of co-operation with the other Nordic countries and particularly with Sweden. Especially after the Baltic countries had been annexed to the Soviet Union and after the economic and cultural impact of Germany in the area of the Baltic Sea had weakened, the Nordic countries – Finland, Sweden, Norway, Denmark and Iceland – drew even closer together. This was expressed by the formation of the Nordic Council, which is an inter-parliamentary body, and many other organs for co-operation particularly in the fields of culture and administration.

The 1960's meant closer economic ties between Finland and Sweden as the movements of the labour force and capital grew quickly, as did trade between the two countries. Finland and Sweden are bound together by innumerable individual and family relationships, cultural ties and a number of joint associations, youth organizations and enterprises. Swedish is still the second national language in Finland and, from the 1960's onwards, every Finnish child has had to learn its basics at school. After the migration from Finland to Sweden in the 1960's Finnish has had a more prominent position in Sweden. Air traffic and particularly boat traffic between Stockholm and Helsinki and Turku and over the Gulf of Bothnia has increased and thousands of people and dozens or hundreds of lorries are carried over every day.

The close relationship between Finland and Sweden as well as between Finland and the other

Nordic countries is also expressed in the co-operation between the main political parties. This co-operation reflects the similarity of the Nordic societies and, at the same time, strengthens their cohesion.

Despite the differences, development has gone towards the so-called welfare state in the creation of which the wealthy Sweden, having been spared the war, had a start over the other Nordic countries and in part also acted as an example. The national solidarity in Finland is, however, partly based on other values, particularly on the efforts during and after the war, so that the general trend in Finnish development has been slower and more conservative than that of Sweden. Correspondingly its construction has been based on greater internal unity, which has been expressed at the political level by continuous coalition governments.

The fast urbanization and industrialization of the country during the 1950's created internal tensions not without foreign policy implications, which were brought to the fore in the 1956 presidential election. In the electoral college Kekkonen, the candidate for the Agrarian Party won by the smallest possible majority (151–149) over the Social Democrat Fagerholm. In the final stage of the election the former received the support of the People's Democrats and the latter of the Conservatives and Liberals. From the point of view of foreign policy Kekkonen was considered a symbol of the Paasikivi doctrine, whereas Fagerholm was considered the representative of the Nordic-western doctrine even though the differences in fact were hardly very great. During Kekkonen's first term of office, first in 1958 with Fagerholm as Prime Minister and later in 1961, Soviet concern over the reflection of great power politics was expressed twice but both times doubts were overcome.

Finland was in fact the only country involved in the second world war which completely fulfilled its obligations to repay the war debt. War reparations had to be paid in the form of industrial goods and this led to a great extent to a change in Finnish industry's production structure and the renewal of machinery. The importance of the metal industry in particular grew greatly and it developed from a home market industry to an export industry. The traditional export industry, wood processing, expanded and was modernized rapidly and exports to western countries began soon after the war. In 1961, in order to secure the preconditions of its most important industry, Finland joined EFTA, the European Free Trade Association, and later in 1973 made an extensive customs agreement with the European Economic Community. On both occasions the country was able to secure its economic interests and still emphasize its independence of the political ties of these economic organizations. The agreement with the EEC was followed by a customs agreement with the East European COMECON. The profound political changes in the Soviet Union/Community of Independent States, Germany and the East bloc caused the EFTA-countries to renegotiate their ties with the European Union in the late 1980's and early 1990's and subject to popular vote Finland became full member of the EU in 1995.

Postwar economic growth continued until 1974, and Finland profited from this fully, although the immediate postwar years were a difficult time, marked by large investments and the payment of war reparations. Industrial reform was followed

Finnish urban growth in the 1960s gave rise to large new housing areas, but the traditional link with the forest was preserved almost everywhere.

from the 1950's on by major infrastructural improvements. The modernization of this large and sparsely-populated country was achieved in a remarkably short time, with the construction of a modern road network, electrification, the introduction of regular domestic flights and an extensive programme of housing construction, particularly in towns. This was followed in the 1960's by a phase of rapid development in social security, and in the system of schools and higher education. All these changes served both to increase national prosperity and to reduce social and regional disparities.

While Finland in the 1930's was still a very agrarian country, its great period of urbanization and industrialization was late compared to that of many other countries and was correspondingly rather fast. This was naturally reflected in political life as well as in the development of attitudes and ideologies. The housing and placing in productive life of the Karelians and those returning from the front was to be confronted immediately after the war. As the towns and industry could not yet employ all this group, a great number of them were settled in smallholdings but these proved to be of little worth and played their part in the new great period of migration in the 1960's. Despite the efforts of the Agrarian and People's Democratic Parties in particular to improve the standard of living in the poor areas of eastern and northern Finland, life could not be improved there without great agricultural subsidies. When, after the 1966 election, the Social Democrats became the leading government party the rationalization of agriculture was carried out. This meant putting an end to particularly unprofitable smallholdings in northern Finland. The consequence was great migration to the towns of southern Finland and to Sweden whose expanding industry at that time needed a great deal of manpower. Understandably this »great migration» caused a lot of social problems and was also reflected very noticably in Finnish literature. The vigorous and popular literary genre of novels and epic literature concentrated for a long time on describing the mental impact of this period of change.

The competition between towns and rural areas, consumers and producers, industry and agriculture has governed Finnish post-war politics – a fact that has not been without foreign policy implications either. As real as competition, however, was the fact that the Social Democrats and the Agrarians together formed a coalition government up till 1987, never on their own it is true, but always as if softened by the inclusion of smaller parties. The authority and often concrete political leadership of the President of the Republic has been a very real part of the politics of compromise within the government, as has the constitutional statutory majority regulations which demand a 2/3 or even 5/6 majority in parliament for the most important bills. The coalitions have been different at the level of local politics. The National Coalition Party was, with the exception of two short periods, an opposition party at the national level till 1987 but was at the local level and particularly in larger towns a dominant party and often in coalition with the Social Democrats.

After the first post-war (1945) election the People's Democrats, which gained a great popularity, took part in government together with the Agrarians and Social Democrats. This was of great significance during the period of major changes; the participation of the People's Democrats in the government brought many advantages to the workers but at the same time prevented extensive strikes and demonstrations. In 1948, after the events in Czechoslovakia, President Paasikivi nominated a Social Democrat minority government led by Fagerholm. This government lasted for about two years despite the suspicions of the Soviet Union and was followed by a number of coalition governments led by Urho Kekkonen as Prime Minister in which the Agrarians were the leading party. When, in 1956, Kekkonen became President he, in turn, nominated his competitor Fagerholm as Prime Minister, but this government came up against internal difficulties, mainly caused by the Soviet Union's suspicions during the stifling Cold War. After the Soviet Union had stopped trade and having called their Ambassador home, the coalition government broke up and the Social Democratic Party split into two for a long time. Only after the 1966 election did the re-united Social Democrats become the leading government party and in addition to the Agrarians the People's Democrats too were in the government. This reflected President Kekkonen's striving for national unification which, during the period of social changes, was as important as immediately after the war. The Communists, however, did not remain in the government for long and during the 1970's their periods in the government compared to the Social Democrats and Agrarians were short. At the beginning of the 1980's support for the Communist Party declined rapidly.

At the end of the 1960's a new protest party came into being alongside the People's Democrats. The smallholders' or Rural Party (Vennamo), representing the outlying districts of eastern Finland, even became a government party in the 1980's. The longest-standing small party in the government has been the Swedish Party, but the Liberal Party, which was often a government party in the 1950's and 1960's, was faced with a crisis in the 1970's and withered away during the 1980's. The opposition generally comprised the People's Democrats-Communists on the one hand and the National Coalition Party on the other. The Finnish government was thus one of the centre-left with the balance changing at times.

After the parliamentary election in 1987, President Koivisto brought the National Coalition Party, which for a long time had been in opposition, into the Government. Harri Holkeri of the National Coalition Party formed a coalition cabinet which conformed to the conventional pattern, except for the fact that the main non-socialist party this time was the National Coalition Party instead of the Centre Party. The Government engaged in the realization of privatization and tax reform following the example of other countries, but the release of foreign exchange trading together with the upswing in trade conditins brought about also in Finland a phase of economic overheat and a so-called casino economy, and the Government was unable to achieve its aim to keep the structural change »under control».

The advantage of the coalition governments has been the securing of large representation of different groups in society. On the other hand, this has often resulted in compromises and costly situations. Government by coalition, in the post-oil crisis period, became under the leadership of President Kekkonen government by consensus. Society had become stabilized after the great migration and youth unrest, and under the external pressure by the price-development of industry. Finland moved into a period of successful economic policy whose aim was, by supporting industry and its competitiveness, to maintain employment and economic growth. Thus the modernization of production carried out in Finland largely under the leadership of the left was completed earlier and more succesfully than in most European countries and based on a broad mutual national understanding.

Finland as most European market economy countries experienced in the late 1980's a period of economic boom associated with a wave of speculation. Finland managed for a long time to preserve the high value of its currency the mark and increased its prosperity with regard to its neighbouring countries as well. The foreign indebtedness of Finland remained for a long time lower than that of many other countries, and the natural debt could be reduced. The private sector committed itself more than ever to the international world by means of its proprietary and debt relationships. The technological modernization of industry and many other soctors maintained the international competitiveness of Finland but, on the other hand, the national economy of Finland began through the influence of integration forces to appear rather low. During the period 1990–1991, however, development turned into a decline in Europe as a whole, and it reflected considerably on Finland, dependent on its export revenues. The shipbuilding industry, which had been successful for a long time, ran into difficulties, and Finland's dependency on the wood processing industry and the engineering industry relative to wood processing was again accentuated. Associated with this was the uncer-tainty about the preserva-

During his extended presidency, Urho Kekkonen,
here in the company of Prime Minister Macmillan,
met many of the world's leaders, conveying the message
of Finland's independence and initiative with
his sharp intelligence, consistent policies
and panache.

tion of natural resources, emphasized by the growing environmental consciousness of the 1980's. Finland's dependency on the outside world also in terms of environmental inconveniences has often become evident. The military risk effect of e.g. Leningrad and the Kola Peninsula regions had to make room in the minds of the Finns for the danger to the environment.

The positive economic development from the end of the 1970's has also had great significance as far as the external esteem of the country is concerned. Finland's policy of neutrality and its position in the world has not always been easily understood abroad. Extensive and successful state visits by President Kekkonen and by President Koivisto made Finland's position and aims widely known, at the same time extensive cultural and economic co-operation with other countries brought a lot of visitors to Finland to see the country and its circumstances with their own eyes. Kekkonen was able to see the result of his work when Finland received as guests the heads of state and heads of government of 35 countries who signed the Helsinki agreement in 1975 at the final stage of the European Conference on Security and Co-operation in Europe.

President Koivisto took up where his predecessor had left by engaging in active official state visit policy and was able to contribute to the process of the leaders of the Soviet Union and the United States approaching each other in the late 1980's. Thus, e.g. the negotiations, during which President Bush and President Gorbachev in 1990 agreed on a mutual policy to pursue in respect of the war against Iraq, which broke out the next year, were held in Helsinki and hosted by President Koivisto. President Koivisto acted in conformity with the

Constitution Act as leader in charge of Finnish foreign policy, and the period of international transition, which had begun in 1989, emphasized this task.

In Finland as elsewhere the post-war great age groups went to school in the 1950's and to universities and other institutes of higher education at the end of the 1960's. The ideological and moral change of the age was strongly felt as was the above-mentioned wave of urbanization which took place at the same time. In university politics a great decentralization programme had already been initiated which was far-reaching in Finland and was followed by strict *numerus clausus*-policy. The period of political consensus has corresponded to peaceful academic and cultural life in which society has favoured above all »useful» and applied teaching and research. Demands have been made, however, on behalf of more ideological debate and criticism and since the 1980's Finnish cultural life has once again begun to orientate itself towards its roots in classical Europe. The development of Europe and Finland in the early 1990's accentuated these orientations rapidly.

President Kekkonen was re-elected to office in 1962, in 1968, in 1974 and in 1978. In addition to his own Agrarian Party he gained support first from the left and then from the right and finally from almost everybody. After he had fallen ill in 1981 (he died in 1986), the Social Democrat Prime Minister, Mauno Koivisto, was elected President in 1982. In addition to his own party he was supported by some of the People's Democrats and many non-socialist supporters and was elected to office by a greater majority than any previous President under normal circumstances. The tradition of coalition government between the Social Democrats, the Agrarians and the small parties continued till 1987, when the National Coalition Party and the Social Democrats formed a coalition government with Harri Holkeri as Prime Minister. President Koivisto was elected for a new term of office in 1988.

The Holkeri Coalition Cabinet was dissolved as a consequence of the parliamentary election in the spring 1991, and a new government was formed on the basis of the election winners, the Centre Party and the National Coalition Party, with the support of the Swedish People's Party and the Finnish Christian League. Esko Aho, the 36-year old Chairman of the Centre Party, was nominated Prime Minister. Due to the difficulty of the economic situation, the Minister of Finance, Iiro Viinanen, the most important cabinet member of the National Coalition Party, gained a very prominent position as well. Despite Finland's relative prosperity and success during this period, Finns bore in mind the lessons of the war and hard times, resorting to a certain »national egotism».

Postwar life in Finland conformed for a long time to the basic configuration that Finland in terms of its cultural nature, its social system and the major part of its foreign trade belonged to the Nordic countries and the »Western» or »market economy» countries while it was making particular efforts to maintain its good political and trade relations with the Soviet Union. It was supporting and promoting all attempts to relieve tension between the superpowers and strengthen the independence of small nations. On its own part, it emphasized the significance of its own national culture and economy, its active foreign policy and efficient defence forces; these important priorities are in Finland generally

Finns have a perhaps somewhat naive enthusiasm for new technology, and are always quick to acquire new appliances. This reflects, on the one hand, the weakness of the old handicrafts tradition and, on the other, a general infatuation with modernity, sometimes referred to as the Japanese-American syndrome. In 1989, at about the time this photo was taken, Finland had the world's highest number of computers in relation to population. Finland's accession to the European Union, a hot topic at the time, was seen analogously as primarily an economic and technological issue.
The boys are playing computer games; the word printed on the girl's T-shirt is *Europa*.

adopted and supported by all social groups. Like all small countries, however, Finland was sensitive to sudden fluctuations in international politics and economy and, on a long-term basis, to cultural development trends.

Finland enhanced its defensive capability by ordering some sixty super-effective – and expensive

– fighter planes in 1992, despite the financial straits in which the government found itself. During the process of disintegration of the Soviet Union, Finland avoided abrasive foreign policy statements on the Baltic countries, stressing that it could not offer security guarantees to its neighbours, which were gaining their independence at the time. To this extent, official Finnish policy differed from the more rhetorical approach of the Swedish and Danish governments. All the more important, Finland reinforced its cultural ties with Estonia, in particular. Humanitarian aid was provided in the midst of the economic crisis by both the government and a wide range of non-governmental organizations. After the Soviet Union had ceased to exist as a political entity, President Koivisto in 1991 unilaterally declared the 1948 Treaty on Friendship, Cooperation and Mutual Assistance to have lapsed.

By the latter half of the 1990's, Estonia and Russia had become significant economic players from the Finnish point of view. Trade with Russia, which had petered out to a mere trickle in the interim years, began to revive rapidly, although the new trade was set up on a completely different basis than the previous centralized system. A particularly important component in this new trade consisted of sales by Finnish consumer goods outlets and department stores to Russian private citizens, while the general focus in Finnish-Russian trade shifted to the St. Petersburg region.

The period between 1989 and 1993 was strongly influenced by the dramatic change undergone by the Soviet Union, the Warsaw Pact Countries and Germany since the autumn 1989. The Government of Finland tried to calm down discussion about joining EC until the EEA Convention gained effect.

In the summer 1991 an unsuccesful coup d'état took place in Moscow and led to the abolishment of the Union of Soviet Socialist Republics towards the end of the year. At that stage, Finland submitted its membership application to EC in 1992.

In 1989, in accordance with the Maastricht Treaty, the European Communities became the European Union. Consequently, membership negotiations now applied to accession to a new, closer union. The EEA Agreement took effect after some delay, in January 1994. In this year, the Treaties of Accession negotiated by the governments of the new applicants were submitted to approval by referendum. Of the EEA countries, Switzerland and Norway opted to remain outside the Union, whereas the people of Austria, Finland (with a 57% majority) and Sweden (with a 52% majority) voted in favour of accession. The political bodies of the three countries went on to confirm the result. Some Finns had misgivings about EU membership on account of nationalist views or for reasons connected with Finland's policy towards Russia, while supporters tended to place the emphasis on the economic benefits and greater security offered by membership. Presumably a great many Finns were swayed in favour of the EU by their wish to emphasize Finland's position within the general European cultural heritage, fearing a false perception of their country and people if it failed to join the Union. Unlike some Norwegians, even those Finns who opposed membership made no attempt to deny the significance of European civilization or to 'scare off' people with the threat of Catholicism.

In the internal affairs of Finland, the change in world order resulted both in modifications in the political world and, more commonly, in cultural

Poster for the EU referendum:
»Yes! women will decide!»

changes facilitated by factors inherent in the deep structures of culture. On the political level, President Koivisto transferred the emphases on the president-centred exercise of power towards the Government and the Prime Minister. A new kind of political tradition emerged in the presidential elections of the late winter 1994, now held without electors in the form of a direct two-phased election. In the primary elections and the first polling round, the voters disregarded the chairmen of the political parties and the political leaders of long-term influence. Rising to the second round, instead of the candidates of the National Coalition Party and the Centre Party, was Mrs. Elisabeth Rehn, of the Swedish People's Party, who had won popularity as »the world's first woman Minister of Defence». The winner of the election by an approx. 54 per cent majority was Martti Ahtisaari, candidate of the Social Democrats, Secretary of State of the Ministry for Foreign Affairs, who had been neither a member of parliament nor a cabinet minister and had the merits of a significant career in international organizations, particularly in the United Nations, and such loose ties to the Party that he received twice the votes of the general support of the Social Democrats. Brought up in the election debate instead of party politics were topics relative to international affairs, humanity and, surprisingly enough, religion; the principal candidates agreed wholeheartedly about many important issues, particularly on the desirability of Finland joining the European Union.

After the heady economic growth of the '80s, from 1990 on the Finnish economy plunged headlong into a deepening recession. Almost complete deregulation of the money market had resulted in increased borrowing by the government, businesses and private individuals, acting on the assumption of continued growth. The ensuing economic retrenchment made the debt a major public – and private – problem, leaving many major and minor economic players bankrupt, and trapping the entire banking system in a serious crisis. The government came to the rescue by taking over the liabilities of the insolvent banks, and was able to prevent many private and business debacles and complete economic chaos at the cost of a growing public debt and a high rate of taxation. Meanwhile, the unemployment rate rose rapidly to nearly 20% of the working-age population; at the time of writing (early 1997), it had remained almost at this level for several years. Unemployment has brought financial worries and identity problems to many individuals and families, and has seriously strained the national economy; nonetheless, Finland has held on to the fundamental principles of the welfare state, averting the real pauperization of the jobless.

Among the major reasons for the crisis were the sudden and unexpected halt to trade with the Soviet Union and the excessive debt contracted during the boom years; high unemployment was also caused in part by the high cost of labour, leading to the rapid and effective automation of production. Inflation came virtually to a standstill, as did the mechanism of annual payrises. The Finnish mark had to be allowed to float from 1992 on, but in 1996 it returned – before the currencies of several other Union countries – to a semi-fixed exchange rate within the Union's exchange-rate mechanism. This decision was preceded by the government's declaration of commitment to the objectives of the Maastricht Treaty and to Finland's participation in the first stage of monetary union. Here, and generally in its relations with the EU, Finland – most explicitly among the countries which joined in 1995 – has pursued a policy aimed at strengthening the Union.

The recession produced changes in the structure of the Finnish economy. Among the most important were several mergers in the forest industry and the banking sector, giving rise to economic units comparable with major European enterprises. At the same time, many public enterprises and utilities were privatized. The period could perhaps be compared with the major economic reforms undertaken in the years 1865–1870, which were accompanied by currency reform, changes in infrastructure occasioning rapid adjustments in the export sector, and famine – and resulted in modernizing Finland's trade and industry, at the cost of great suffering.

Finland was led through the recession and the EEA and EU membership negotiations by President Koivisto and a multiparty centre-right coalition government headed by Esko Aho, chairman of the Centre Party, while the Social Democrats and the Left-Wing Alliance were in the opposition. The economic crisis and the major national issue of EU membership, however, prompted far-reaching solidarity between the government, the opposition and the labour market. Following parliamentary elections in 1995, a new multiparty government took power. Headed by Paavo Lipponen, chairman of the Social Democratic Party, it included virtually all the major parties from right to left, except the Centre Party. This government has followed the economic course charted by its predecessor – its Finance Minister, like that of the previous government, is a member of the Conservative Party. Its main goals have been to bring the public debt under control, stimulate economic activity, fight inflation and cut costs.

The position of Finland on the periphery of Europe, but nevertheless close to its important borders and in the sphere of various influences, has compelled Finland to delve into history, to find there the continuity of settlement and production, on the one hand, and the influence of great changes in world politics, on the other hand, and to assess its own ability to meet these time-imposed challenges.

The tradition of the Swedish rule lies deep in the structure of Finland, its social system and world of concepts. The tradition of the Grand Duchy era and subsequent relations with Russia stays alive in the sense that the Finns have a way of thinking internationally and realistically. Inherent in the republic tradition are the perseverance and spirit of self-sacrifices displayed in times of war and difficulties, and the sense of solidarity in a tight spot. The new phase in the history of Europe that opened in 1989 has been reflected clearly in Finland's position, which is now more in the geopolitical centre of things than before. This is due to an eastward shift in European affairs as a result of upheavals in Germany and the emergence of the Baltic region as a new, active force; Finland's accession to the European Union also contributed to the change. Meanwhile, the significance of Nordic cooperation has waned since the days of the Cold War. The disintegration of the Soviet Union and change in Russia have also affected Finland's status. From Finland's viewpoint, Russia remains an important neighbour whose every step must be watched closely. Meanwhile, as a member of the European Union, Finland must now carry a greater responsibility than before

Presidential inauguration in 1994:
Mrs Riitta Uosukainen, Speaker of Parliament and former teacher of Finnish, listening to the parting words of the resigning President Mauno Koivisto; on the right, Martti Ahtisaari, the new President of the Republic. The presidents bear the insignia of the three national orders. On the left, three official flags bearing the Finnish coat of arms; behind the flags, Wäinö Aaltonen's sculpture idealizing motherhood.

for relatively distant issues, such as those involving the Mediterranean region and the Balkans.

The many changes and crises Finland has gone through in the past have equipped us with the capacity to find new solutions and adjust to new situations in world politics. At the same time, Finns are as aware as ever today of the importance of fostering the social, moral and cultural values implicit in the common European heritage. All these features may, however, well be considered to constitute parts of the general European social and moral culture, to which Finland has belonged for almost a millennium.

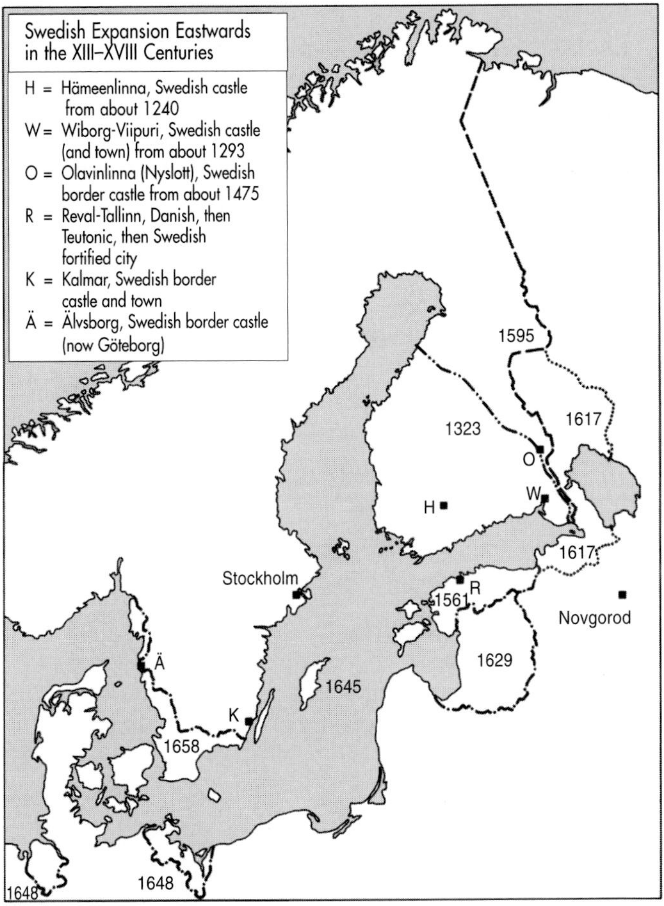
Swedish Expansion Eastwards in the XIII–XVIII Centuries
H = Hämeenlinna, Swedish castle from about 1240
W = Wiborg-Viipuri, Swedish castle (and town) from about 1293
O = Olavinlinna (Nyslott), Swedish border castle from about 1475
R = Reval-Tallinn, Danish, then Teutonic, then Swedish fortified city
K = Kalmar, Swedish border castle and town
Ä = Älvsborg, Swedish border castle (now Göteborg)
1595
1617
1323
O
W
H
1617
Stockholm
R
1561
Novgorod
1629
Ä
1645
K
1658
1648
1648

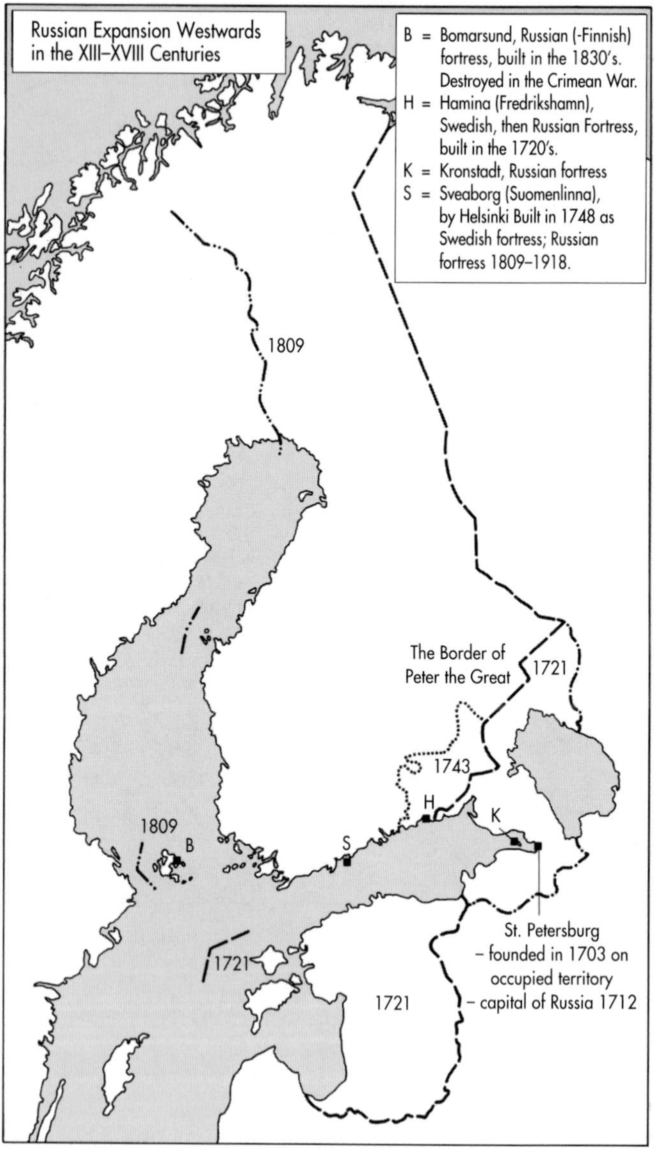
Russian Expansion Westwards
in the XIII–XVIII Centuries
B = Bomarsund, Russian (-Finnish) fortress, built in the 1830's. Destroyed in the Crimean War.
H = Hamina (Fredrikshamn), Swedish, then Russian Fortress, built in the 1720's.
K = Kronstadt, Russian fortress
S = Sveaborg (Suomenlinna), by Helsinki Built in 1748 as Swedish fortress; Russian fortress 1809–1918.
1809
The Border of
Peter the Great
1721
1743
H
K
S
1809
B
St. Petersburg
– founded in 1703 on occupied territory
– capital of Russia 1712
1721
1721

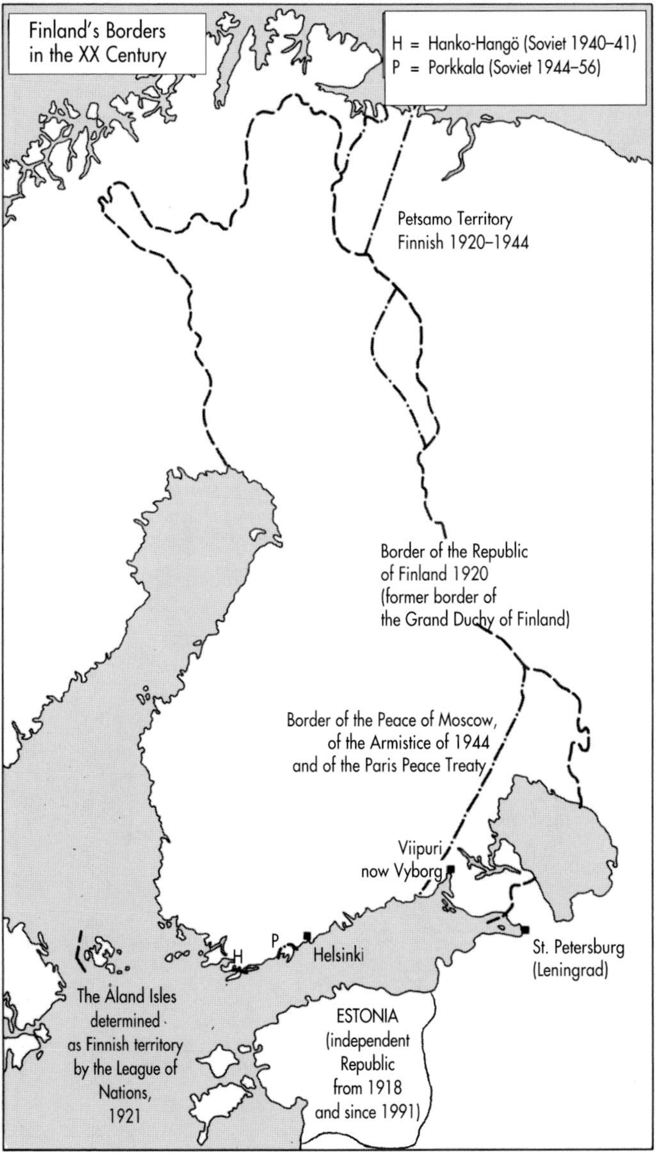
Finland's Borders
in the XX Century
H = Hanko-Hangö (Soviet 1940–41)
P = Porkkala (Soviet 1944–56)
Petsamo Territory
Finnish 1920–1944
Border of the Republic
of Finland 1920
(former border of
the Grand Duchy of Finland)
Border of the Peace of Moscow,
of the Armistice of 1944
and of the Paris Peace Treaty
Viipuri
now Vyborg
H
P
Helsinki
St. Petersburg
(Leningrad)
The Åland Isles
determined
as Finnish territory
by the League of
Nations,
1921
ESTONIA
(independent
Republic
from 1918
and since 1991)

PHOTOGRAPHS:

Otava picture archives and
Department of Museums pp. 42, 80, 100, 105, 142;
Finnish Army pp. 131, 133;
Finnish Literature Society p. 73;
Helsinki City Museum pp. 68, 106;
Tove Jansson p. 134;
Matti Klinge's archives pp. 39–41;
Lehtikuva pp. 136, 139, 157, 168, 171;
Olaus Magnus, *Pohjoisten kansojen historia*
(History of the Northern Peoples) p. 29
O. A. Mankell p. 81;
National Museum of Finland pp. 54–57, 83, 88, 97;
Stefan (Tapani Kovanen) 146;
Z. Topelius, *Finland framstäldt i techningar*
(Finland Represented in Drawings), pp. 18, 66, 84.